Capo Voodoo Gu

SECRETS OF PARTIAL CAPOS IN DADGAD TUNING

Unlocking Another Dimension in Your Guitar

HARVEY REID

Woodpecker Multimedia

York, Maine USA

www.PartialCapo.com

© 2012-2014 by Harvey Reid

*In memory of Jefferson H. Hickey, who understood, and
for Lyle Shabram, who started it all*

ISBN: 978-1-63029-007-8

PO Box 815 York Maine 03909 USA

www.woodpecker.com

CONTENTS

About This Book	2
Why A Partial Capo in DADGAD Tuning?	3
Partial Capo Hardware	5
About the Diagrams in This Book	7
Chord Voicings & Inversions	8
Some Partial Capo Math...	9

1- "Top 4 @2"		[0 0 2 2 2 2]	11
2- "Bottom 4 @2"		[2 2 2 2 0 0]	15
3- "Bottom 3 @2"		[2 2 2 0 0 0]	18
4- "Esus"		[0 2 2 2 0 0]	21
5- "Open A"		[0 0 2 2 2 0]	24
6- "Middle 4 @2"		[0 2 2 2 2 0]	27
7- "Faux-Standard"		[2 0 0 0 2 2]	29
8- "Bottom 5 @3"		[3 3 3 3 3 0]	31
9- "Top 4 @3"		[0 0 3 3 3 3]	34
10- "Open A @3"		[0 0 3 3 3 0]	37
11- "Bottom 5 @4"		[4 4 4 4 4 0]	40
12- "Middle 4 @4"		[0 4 4 4 4 0]	42
13- "Middle 2 @4"		[0 0 4 4 0 0]	44
14- "Top 5 @5"		[0 5 5 5 5 5]	44
15- "Esus @5"		[0 5 5 5 0 0]	48
16- "Bottom 2 @5"		[5 5 0 0 0 0]	50
17- "Top 5 @7"		[0 7 7 7 7 7]	53
18- "Top 4 @7"		[0 0 7 7 7 7]	55
19- "Bottom 4 @7"		[7 7 7 7 0 0]	57
20- 024440		[0 2 4 4 4 0]	61
21- 777740		[7 7 7 7 4 0]	63
22- 553330		[5 5 3 3 3 0]	66
23- 550030		[5 5 0 0 3 0]	68
24- High G- Low C	[CGDGAD]	[0 0 0 0 0 5]	70
25- "Add-Gad"	[CGDGAD]	[2 2 0 0 0 0]	73
26- "Top 5 @5"	[CGDGAD]	[0 5 5 5 5 5]	76
27- "Top 4 @5"	[CGDGAD]	[0 0 5 5 5 5]	78
APPENDIX: Comparing DADGAD to E-Suspended (Esus)			80
About the Author			99

About This Book

Partial capos are commonly thought of as an alternative to open tunings. Most of the manufacturers of partial capos advertise them as a way to play in open tunings, which is actually quite misleading, since capos do not really change the tuning. Partial capo users generally also view them as a tuning substitute, often without realizing that you can combine the two ideas and use them in any tuning.

Over the last several decades, DADGAD has become an "established" guitar tuning, and players around the world are developing considerable skill and familiarity with it. Players who use tunings often perform in a wide variety of tunings, but the guitarists who play in DADGAD often make a more serious "commitment" to learning the tuning for more than just a song or two. This makes it an attractive subject for some deeper partial capo explorations.

If you give a partial capo to a guitar player, there is no certainty that they will find musical uses for it. How to effectively use a partial capo is by no means obvious, even to a skilled guitarist. The man who invented, patented and manufactured the first partial capo never discovered any of the common musical uses of it. I had one of his capos for several years before it occurred to me to use the *Esus* configuration, which is now my favorite partial capo idea. The knowledge of what strings to capo, as well as the understanding of where to put your fingers– is vitally important and hard to figure out. After you have done it for a while the partial capo idea becomes "obvious," and you then wonder why everyone has not been using them all along.

This book contains over 800 chords, and shows you 25 different ways to play music with various kinds of partial capos, mostly in DADGAD tuning, with a few in the related CGDGAD tuning. The ideas here should enable a player of any level to find a lot of new and useful musical sounds, saving a lot of effort finding the capo configurations and fingerings. Beginners as well as professionals can immediately start making new music with the skills they already have. There are new places for your fingers, and new sounds when you put your fingers in familiar places.

Thousands of partial capos owners have discovered that there is very little information to be found about where to put the capos and where to put their fingers. The various partial capos made by *Shubb*, *SpiderCapo* and *Kyser* essentially have no instructions, and the people who make them give no hint that they are useful in anything but standard tuning. The instruction sheet for the *Third Hand* capo (something I wrote in the early 1980's, and for over 30 years the best single source of information about partial capos) only shows a total of 85 chords in 20 different capo configurations, with no mention of using them in DADGAD tuning.

The vast majority of guitarists do not read music, and no one reads notes in open tunings, so written arrangements are of little use. Few songs are widely-known any more, so I filled the **Capo Voodoo** books with chords rather than song arrangements. Try the chords, listen to what they can do, and put them to use in your own music. It's a valuable music theory lesson to study the chord structure of these chords, since each is shown with its voicing and inversion information spelled out. The letter names of each note are shown for every chord, along with the scale positions they occupy with respect to the root note of the chord.

Because you can always play barre chords above the capo, I did not show you all the chords on the guitar. **This book is by no means a complete encyclopedia of all chords, and you'll need to do more exploring.** You may find valuable things on your own, and there are other ways to use partial capos that are not covered in this book. The idea was to show you chords that are good examples of the new sounds you can get with partial capos, and fingerings that best illustrate the strengths and advantages of each capo configuration. In general, the more chords I have included, the more musically interesting I think each configuration is.

You'll still have to do some work finding the corresponding scale patterns, and to write and arrange your own music using these ideas. Not all songs work well with a partial capo, and it takes skill, time and luck to find the ones that really shine. The chords shown here should get you started, and hopefully will point you in new directions toward other chords and chord voicings you can use for your own music.

The information in this book should help guitarists find the amazing sounds that have been hiding in their fingerboards. This book should also make it clear to skeptics that the world of partial capos is much larger and more musically valuable than anyone has previously imagined.

Why A Partial Capo?

The partial capo, often called a "cut capo," is a quick and easy way to change the limits of what is possible on the guitar. It is most useful in solo guitar situations, where the added resonance of having an extra string or two ringing can be dramatic. The reasons that guitarists have found value in different tunings are basically the same reasons you use a partial capo, and they both offer new but not identical landscapes of voicings, scales, chord possibilities and open-string resonances.

The basic idea of the partial capo is that it presents a new set of open-strings, just as a different tuning does, but it works differently. People generally use a partial capo to avoid playing in different tunings, and if you stay in any tuning and use capos, the geometry of your scale and chord fingerings remain familiar. Any time you change the tuning, the mapping of notes onto the fingerboard changes. With partial capos, chords and notes remain where they usually are, but you get new open strings and some different notes added to familiar chords. The kinds of rich, droning sounds we associate with tunings are available, and yet another set of them appear whenever you combine capos and tunings.

It is much less understood that you can also use partial capos in any tuning. Each tuning offers a unique library of ways to play chords and scales. The positions, scales and the lifetime of left-hand fingerings you learn are changed each time you change the tuning. The scale and chord fingerings change as well as the open strings. Partial capos allow you to apply whatever in-depth knowledge you have of your favorite tuning to a new set of sounds. Players who change tunings for every song can't really take advantage of their knowledge of the fingerboard the way you can if you stay in one tuning and use partial capos.

Don't be surprised if you get confused by partial capos. Many great guitarists have been!

Singers & songwriters can find new chords & chord voicings, and fresh ways to accompany & arrange songs.

Advanced players can do amazing things with a partial capo, and play complex music that would be impossible otherwise.

This book shows dozens of ways to use partial capos in DADGAD tuning, and guides you through the confusing landscape of new possibilities.

There are millions of ways to put partial capos on a guitar, but only a handful are really musically useful.

Partial capos are usually seen as a substitute for playing in a non-standard tuning. Using partial capos in combination with another tuning is exciting and unexplored.

A Liberty "Flip" Model 43 partial capo clamping 4 strings at fret 2.

Shubb and Kyser 3-string "ESUS" capos clamping strings at 2 different frets.

Partial Capo Hardware

Partial Capo Hardware

There are now almost 20 models of partial capos that clamp 1 to 5 strings. Each has unique musical value, and there is no such thing as a "best" partial capo. You will likely find yourself with an assortment of capos that you use for different purposes and different guitars. Universal versions that clamp any combination of strings are the most versatile, but also the most clumsy and obtrusive. Single-purpose partial capos are easier to operate, less noticeable on the guitar, and are generally more desirable because they are less visible and don't get in your way as much when you try to reach over and around them. Not all partial capos will fit the string spacing, neck thickness and action of every guitar, and you won't know for sure if many of them will work for you until you try them on your guitars. Only the *SpiderCapo* allows you to flip the "fingers" up or down in mid-song, though the *Kyser K-Lever* capos let you temporarily clamp strings that lie under the capo.

UNIVERSAL CAPOS

"Third Hand" universal capo

"SpiderCapo" universal capo

3-STRING CAPOS

"Liberty Flip" 3/4-string capo

"Shubb c7b" 3-string capo

Kyser "Short-Cut" 3-string capo

"Liberty Flip" Model 43 capo

"Planet Waves Trio" 4/5-string capo

"Shubb c8b" 5-string capo

4 & 5-STRING "SHORTENED" CAPOS

Kyser "Drop-D" 5-string capo

Planet Waves "Dual-Action" full capo

K-Lever & G-Band Partial Capos

Kyser makes 4 of their "*K-Lever*" capos, developed by Greg O'Haver. They clamp 3, 4 or 5 strings, and then offer the additional option of letting you fret notes under the capo by holding the spring lever down with a spare finger. When you let go of the lever it springs back to its original position.

You can also make your own single-purpose partial capos, most easily by starting with *Shubb* brass capos. They can be cut off easily with a hacksaw (use a razor blade or scissors to cut the rubber) and shaped with a metal file. You may need to use a rat-tail, oval or triangular file to notch out the brass shaft to leave strings room to vibrate. Metals used in most other capos are harder to work with.

KYSER "K-LEVER" GREEN *with spring lever on 1 string. Clamps 5 strings on bass or treble sides, lever clamps one E string.*

KYSER "K-LEVER" RED *"Double-Drop D" clamps 4 inner strings. Lever clamps either E string under the capo.*

KYSER "K-LEVER" BLUE *3-string capo, lever clamps one E string.*

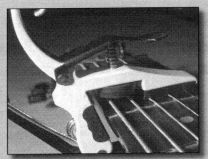
KYSER "K-LEVER" WHITE *clamps 3 inner strings (002220 in this picture) and the lever clamps 2 outer strings. Attaches on opposite side from other Esus capos.*

Woodie's G-Band capos comes in 2 models, that clamp either 1) one of the E strings bass or treble side, or 2) two outer strings on either side. They are made of spring steel coated with soft rubber. You can notch a *Model 2* capo with a razor blade so it clamps only the B string. Barely visible on your fingerboard, and very easy to reach over and around. *G-Band* capos allow things that no other capo can do. They are not adjustable and may not fit narrow, children's, wide-neck, 12-strings, or work properly high up the neck.

A Woodie's G Band Model 1

A Woodie's G Band Model 2 on the bass

About the Diagrams in This Book

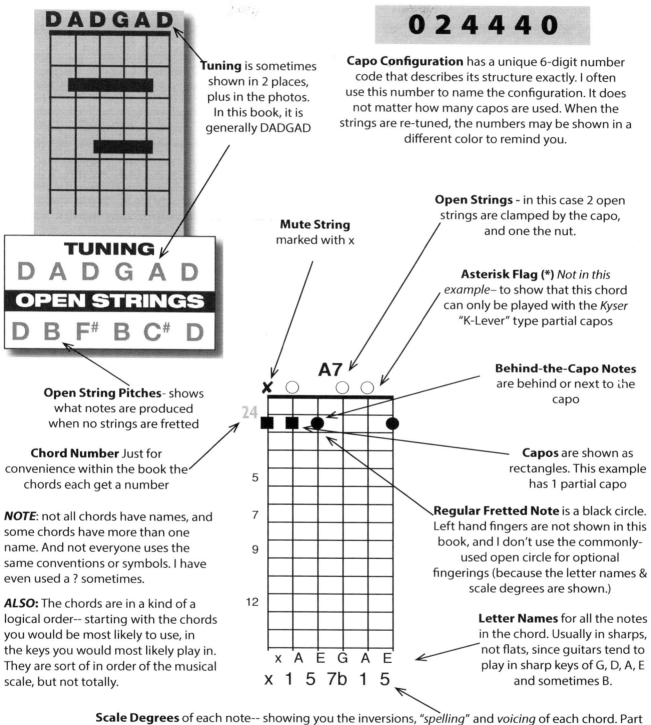

Tuning is sometimes shown in 2 places, plus in the photos. In this book, it is generally DADGAD

Capo Configuration has a unique 6-digit number code that describes its structure exactly. I often use this number to name the configuration. It does not matter how many capos are used. When the strings are re-tuned, the numbers may be shown in a different color to remind you.

Open Strings - in this case 2 open strings are clamped by the capo, and one the nut.

Mute String marked with x

Asterisk Flag (*) *Not in this example*– to show that this chord can only be played with the *Kyser* "K-Lever" type partial capos

Open String Pitches- shows what notes are produced when no strings are fretted

Behind-the-Capo Notes are behind or next to the capo

Chord Number Just for convenience within the book the chords each get a number

Capos are shown as rectangles. This example has 1 partial capo

NOTE: not all chords have names, and some chords have more than one name. And not everyone uses the same conventions or symbols. I have even used a ? sometimes.

Regular Fretted Note is a black circle. Left hand fingers are not shown in this book, and I don't use the commonly-used open circle for optional fingerings (because the letter names & scale degrees are shown.)

ALSO: The chords are in a kind of a logical order-- starting with the chords you would be most likely to use, in the keys you would most likely play in. They are sort of in order of the musical scale, but not totally.

Letter Names for all the notes in the chord. Usually in sharps, not flats, since guitars tend to play in sharp keys of G, D, A, E and sometimes B.

Scale Degrees of each note-- showing you the inversions, *"spelling"* and *voicing* of each chord. Part of what gives each chord its musical identity is determined by which numbers are present. The order in which they appear, and which of them are absent or *doubled* (repeated) is also a vital factor. There are many voicings of any chord, and only some of them are available on a guitar.

In this example, A is the root or 1, so the 5th of an A scale is an E and the flat 7th is a G. These numbers show you the structure and help you analyze and understand the sound of each chord.

Chord Voicings & Inversions

As you flip around this book, you'll see a lot of the same chord names—like D, E7, Em, A. Don't make the natural assumption that there are a lot of duplicates, and look more carefully at the scale numbers on the bottom of each chord diagram. You'll notice that the "spelling" of these different *inversions* and *voicings* are not all the same, and if you compare their sound, a wealth of new harmonic subtlety opens up to you. Because pianos cannot play the same note in duplicate places, there are chord voicings on guitar that cannot be played on a keyboard.

You always have different choices of chord voicings available in any guitar tuning, and how many there are depends on the tuning, the notes that make up that chord, and your left hand agility. (Many beginners fail to see the depth of this idea and think that there is only one E chord and a couple different C chords, for example.) There are actually about 8 playable voicings of an E major chord in standard tuning. If you are reading this book, it probably means that you have some experience with at least one other tuning, and you may already understand that it is a vital part of arranging your music to find the chord voicings that you like for each song.

The partial capo gives you quick access to a vast and diverse world of new chords, as well as a surprisingly large number of new ways of voicing familiar chords. Try to appreciate the complexity of all the choices and sounds that arise from the large number of new inversions and voicings of all sorts of chords, and the new musical opportunities that come with them. There are new chord voicings of common chords here, and completely new harmonies, dissonances and resonances that cannot be achieved any other way. You will probably find that certain voicings of some chords feel just right and others don't, and with some careful experimentation you can bring a world of fresh new ideas to your music. In this book there are 32 unique D chords, and 24 different A chord voicings.

It is a somewhat startling fact that nearly 80% of the chords in this book are unique voicings that occur only once. Many more of them show up only a few times, and very few can be played without a partial capo. For example, chord #9 on page 22 is a 1 1 5 5 2 1 voicing of a *Dadd9* chord. It is the only occurrence, not only in this tuning, but in the entire catalog of nearly 10000 partial capo chords I have assembled in close to 2 dozen tunings and almost 200 partial capo configurations. If you want that chord's particular sound, that's the only way I know to get it.

Once you embrace this new world of harmonic ideas and resonances, your music will never sound the same again.

> **It is a startling fact that 80% of the chords in this book are unique voicings that occur only once.**
>
> **Even more remarkable is that over 3/4 of these chord voicings cannot be played at all in standard tuning. If you have not used tunings or partial capos, there are nearly 800 chords here you have never played on a guitar.**

Some Partial Capo Math...

How Many Partial Capo Configurations Are There?

To figure how many ways you can put a partial capo on a guitar...

We don't count "0 0 0 0 0 0" which is no strings clamped, and we don't count clamping all 6 strings which is a full capo.

If we solve for

- X = the number of configurations
- C = the number of capos
- F = the number of frets on the instrument
- S = the number of strings on the instrument

With a universal capo, each string can be capoed or left open at any fret.

With one capo it is pretty easy...

Just 2 to the S power minus 1, since each of the S strings can be either up or down. So 2 to the 6th power, minus one = 64-1= 63 with at least one string capoed but not all 6.

This means a 6-string guitar yields 63 configurations of one partial capo at each fret. So on a 12 fret neck one universal partial capo can clamp 63 x 12 = **756** configurations, and **882** for a 14-fret neck. It's not easy to get a capo on many guitars at the 14th fret, so it's safe to say **there are 756 ways to put one capo on a guitar, in each tuning.**

It is a lot harder when you use multiple capos, since if more than one capo clamps the same string, only one of them does anything.

"f over c" is "f things taken c at a time" if you remember the formula from math class long ago

$$\text{Then } x = \binom{f}{c}\left[(c+1)^s - 1\right]$$

So with 2 capos we get 66 x 728= **48,048** configurations

and with 3 capos we get = **900,900** configurations

For 12 capos we get = **4,826,808** configurations.

You can also get this same number more easily by thinking like this: The 1st string has 13 different fretting choices on a 12 fret neck (since we count the open string)-- so a 2-string instrument would have (13x13)-1 combinations, and thus a 6-string guitar would have (13x13x13x13x13x13)-1= 4,826,808 configurations. So a 14-fret guitar would yield (15x15x15x15x15x15)-1= 11,390,624 configurations.

This means there are theoretically over 11 million ways to put partial capos on a guitar fingerboard– in every different tuning! Because strings break if you tune them sharp, and they lose tone if you loosen them more than 3-4 frets, the permutations of partial capos is mathematically larger than that of just tunings. There are roughly 5x5x5x5x5x5 tunings (15000+) that you could try with a standard set of strings. I generally find a few dozen useful ways to use capos in each tuning, which leads me to estimate that there are roughly 2000 musically useful capo configurations for every 100 tunings. Since there are about 100 tunings in use, my current research represents about 10-20% of the total size of the "hidden world" of partial capos on a 6-string guitar.

The Chords...

Where to put the capos and how to find the music

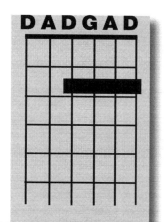

TUNING
DADGAD
OPEN STRINGS
DAEABE

1– "Top 4 @2" 002222

This configuration is a logical starting point, since it is easier to get used to than some later ideas. It is common in partial capoing to leave 1 or 2 of the outer strings uncapoed like this, and add the open bass or treble notes to various chords. In the next example we will flip the capo around to the bottom 4 strings.

Here the open strings give you D A E A B E, which is closely related to the mysterious and lovely C G D G A D tuning probably invented by English guitarist Dave Evans in the 1960's, and recently adopted and popularized by American guitarist El McMeen and some others. If you raised (or capoed that tuning a whole step it would also be D A E A B E. On pages 68-77 we look at ideas for partial capos in CGDGAD tuning.

Probably the best possibilities here involve playing in the key of A, or related modal keys. There are a lot of modal A5 chords, and modal scale patterns also lie conveniently across the fingerboard. In fact, it is easy to play quite a number of modal or "power chords" (chords with no 3rd, that are neither major or minor) in this tuning/configuration, since many of them land conveniently under your fingers (see chord diagrams.) DADGAD tuning allows you to barre anywhere and add one finger above the barre to make a "power chord" such as 444644.

This is a good way to give you some new musical options once you already have your guitar in DADGAD tuning, and it gives a performer a way to do some different-sounding songs without changing the tuning or risking every song having a similar sound. I first saw guitarist Al Petteway using this particular configuration.

The most reliable way to capo just 4 strings is with a *Planet Waves Trio* or a universal capo. There are not many chords that require reaching over the capo, so a universal capo can effectively do this. Depending on the width and shape of your guitar neck you might be able to do this with a *Planet Waves Dual-Action* full capo, and a *Liberty "Flip"* can usually do it also.

A *Third Hand* capo forming a DADGAD Top 4 configuration.

A *Liberty "Flip"* Model 43 capo at the 2nd fret making the 002222 configuration. The capo can also clamp 4 inner strings, or flip over to clamp 3 inner strings.

Focusing this book on DADGAD tuning offers an example of what could be done in any tuning. Since there are hundreds of tunings, thousands of unique chord voicings, and thousands of partial capo configurations, it's clear that no one will ever see the end of the new musical ideas and the exploration.

0 0 2 2 2 2

Some Chords in the DADGAD "Top 4" Configuration p.1
TUNING: DADGAD

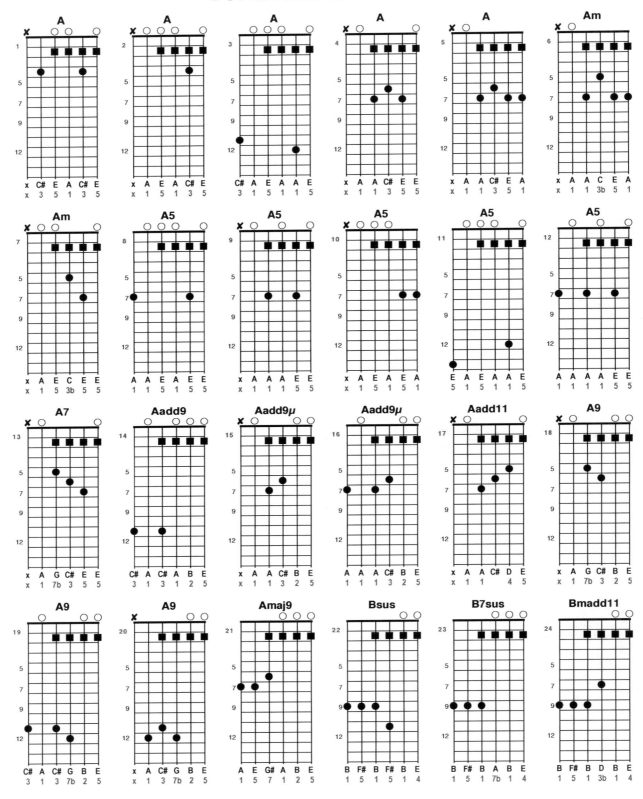

Some Chords in the DADGAD "Top 4" Configuration p.2
TUNING: DADGAD

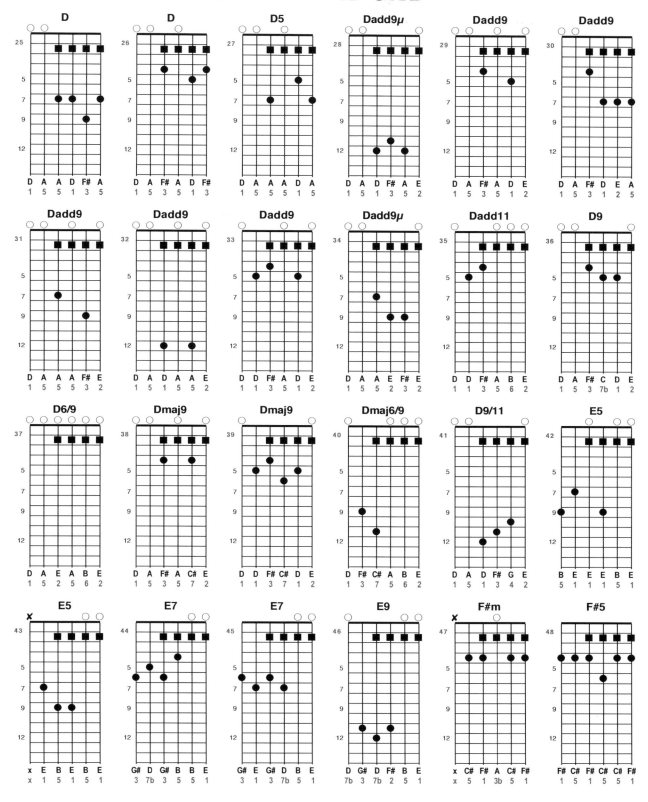

Some Chords in the DADGAD "Top 4" Configuration p.3
TUNING: DADGAD

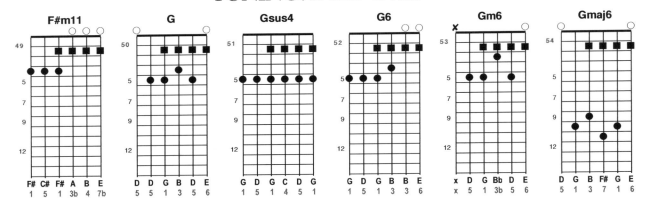

ABOUT "MU" CHORDS

The legendary rock band *Steely Dan* made extensive use of an unusual type of chord that they named the "*mu*" or *μ* chord, and wrote about in their songbook. They are major chords with an added 2nd that also still have the 3rd, and there are really only three that you can play in standard tuning. When both notes are present in the same octave (it is often called an *add2* when you add the 2nd in a lower octave and an *add9* when the added note is an octave higher) there is a lovely effect. These chords have existed on the piano for a long time, but were never given a special name or attention on guitar.

See where the 2 and 3 scale notes are on adjacent strings

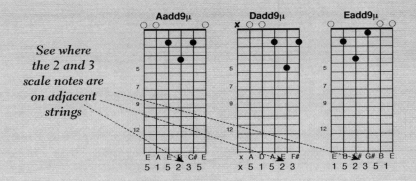

In standard tuning, it is hard to add the 2nd without removing the 3rd. When you use a partial capo, this kind of chords become a lot more common on guitar, and there are over 50 of them scattered around this book (two are on the previous page) that have a 2 and a 3 next to each other. They are often but not always on adjacent strings, and some of the configurations where the capo is in the middle at the 5th or seventh fret mean that one of the treble strings played open or the capo can add this note.

- I have flagged most of them with a Greek letter μ after the chord, and sometimes also "minor mu" chords. I probably should have also made up a symbol and flagged some of the other similarly interesting chord extensions that are scattered around this book, such as with added 4th and 6ths that retain the 3rds and 5ths right next to them. I call chords with the 1-2-3-4-5 notes in them "*9/11*," since they have the 9th (2nd) and the 11th (4th) as well as the 1-3-5. There are quite a few of them in the book.

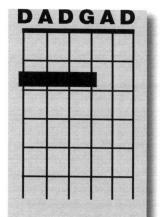

2- "Bottom 4 @2" 222200

This configuration opens up some nice new territory by moving you up a whole step to the key center of E and providing some new options on the treble end. Because the top 2 open strings are part of a D chord, a good bet here is to play modal music in E, which often requires the use of the flat 7 or "drop" chord, which would in this case be a D chord. In regular DADGAD, you don't have many good options for a strong "drop" chord. (Which in the key of D would be a C chord.)

Not only do you have a lot of new and interesting chords, but your scales for fiddle-tune type melodic playing are also very convenient, and this creates a nice solo guitar situation.

You'll also notice a lot of E7 and even some E9 chords, and you could even play a really bluesy song with the E7, A7 and B7 chords you see in the chart here, as well as a very nice voicing of a D7 chord.

There are also quite a number of Bm7 and Bm9 voicings, and you might be able to build a song around them that went to some new and unexpected places.

The most reliable way to capo just 4 strings is with a *Planet Waves Trio* or a universal capo. There are a number of chords and scales (like #1,2,5) where it is helpful to reach over the capo, so a universal capo would not be nearly as useful here. As with the previous example you might be able to do this with a *Planet Waves Dual-Action* full capo or a *Liberty "Flip."*

*A **Planet Waves Trio** capo forming a DADGAD Bottom 4 configuration.*

ABOUT NAMING CHORDS

- **Not all chords have names**, and there is no consistent, widespread naming system in place.

- **Chords are usually named and described according to the "root" note.** It is not always clear what the root note is, and you might use a chord I have called "E-something" as an "A-something" chord, which would give it a different name. So feel free to disagree with the names I give some chords if you hear or use them differently.

- **Some common chords have more than one name.** For example, depending on the root, C6= C-E-G-A and Am7= A-C-E-G have the same notes but in a different order. And a chord with 1-3-5-6 is a 6th chord, but a 1-3-5-6-7^b is also usually just called a 6th; also sometimes a *dominant 6th* or *6/7*. These are called *"enharmonic equivalents."*

- **Omitted and doubled notes** change the sound of chord also, but there is no indication in the name of the chord to show that the 3rd or 5th might be missing, or that there might be three 5's and only one 3.

222200

Some Chords in the DADGAD "Bottom 4" Configuration p.1
TUNING: DADGAD

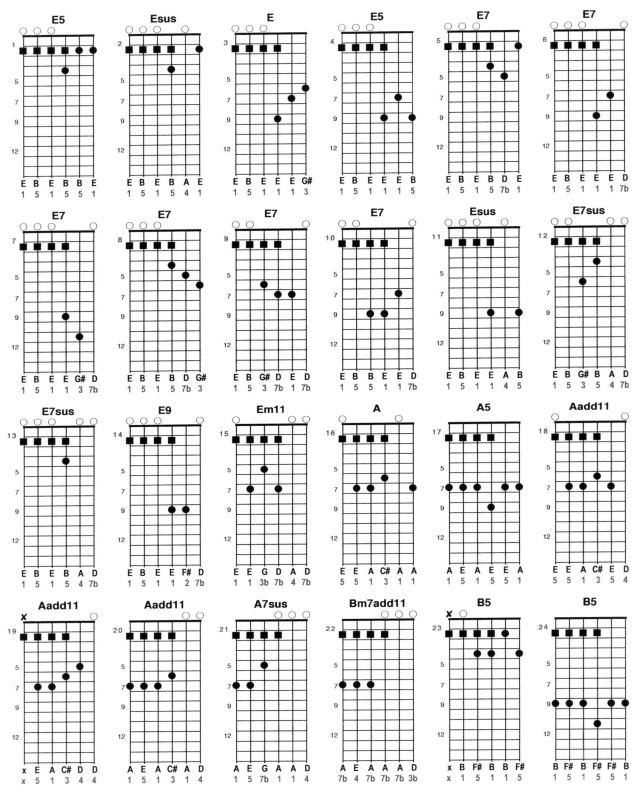

Some Chords in the DADGAD "Bottom 4" Configuration p 2
TUNING: DADGAD

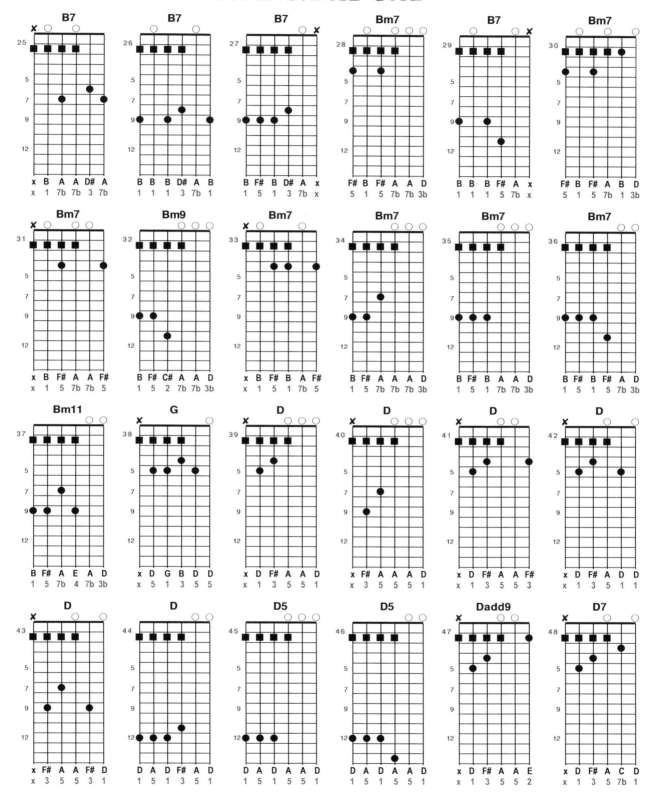

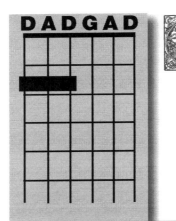

3- "Bottom 3 @2" 222000

There are some great chords here, and like a lot of the configurations in this book, it offers not only a way to get some new chords, but to shift your key center away from D.

Because your bottom 3 strings now form a 1-5-1 in E, it makes sense to center your music there. The top 3 strings add a minor 3rd, an 11th and a 9th, so it is easy to get some complex chord extensions. You'll find some nice Em7 and Em9 chords in the chart (chords #26-38.)

It is also possible to play in A in this situation, and there are also some C and G root chords, so you can play music with some root movement, and you are not stuck droning the tonic chord in the open tuning.

The music that comes out of this configuration seems to want to be jazzier, and there is some nice dissonance and angularity that is quite refreshing.

To capo just 3 strings you need a universal capo, unless you can find a way to shorten an existing capo. You might try cutting off a *Planet Waves Trio*. The result will probably depend on the shape and width of your guitar neck.

A *Third Hand* capo forming a DADGAD 222000 configuration. The side support on the treble end keeps it from tilting over.

Possibly the hardest thing about the partial capo is understanding that it behaves like a tuning but it is not the same thing at all. It is common, and possibly helpful at first to think of many of the capo configurations as being ways to "imitate" the sound of various tunings. This only seems to happen, but since this book is about using capos in DADGAD tuning, you may learn more quickly than players who remain in standard tuning that partial capos are a fundamentally different thing than tunings. They don't work the same way at all, and only a few things can be made to sound identical both ways. The last 20 pages of this book show you how different an Esus partial capo is from the actual DADGAD tuning.

222000

Some Chords in the DADGAD "Bottom 3" Configuration p.1
TUNING: DADGAD

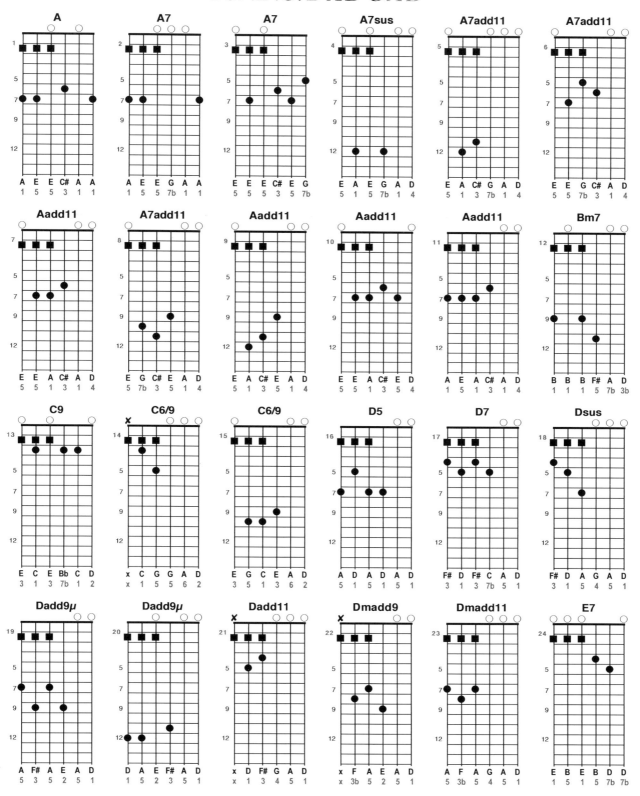

Some Chords in the DADGAD "Bottom 3" Configuration p.2
TUNING: DADGAD

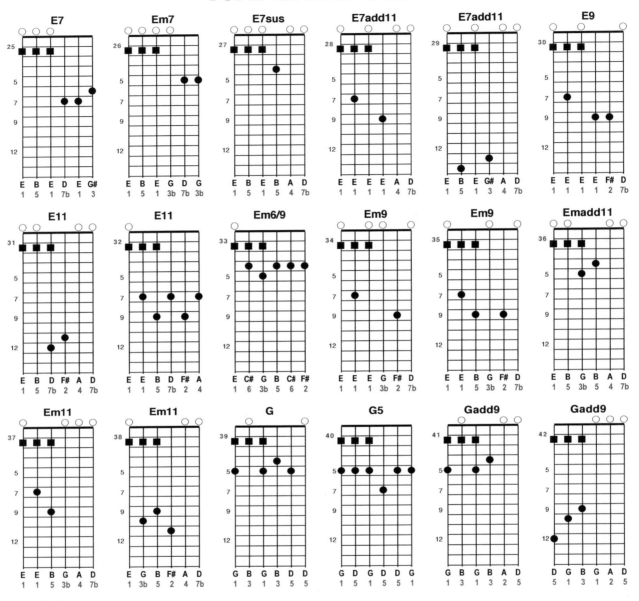

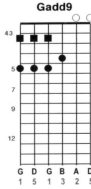

This book by no means represents everything you can do with partial capos, but it should give anyone some good ideas of how they work.

Many guitarists are still skeptical of partial capos, and because they are not convinced of the musical value of the idea, they don't explore much, and pull back when they get confused. Try the capo configurations presented here and listen carefully, and hopefully you'll realize how much good music is waiting to be discovered.

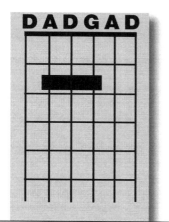

4 – "Esus" 022200

This one uses a 3-string *Esus* capo, which is the most common type of partial capo used in standard tuning. Even though it no longer makes an *Esus* chord, I have chosen to use the name *Esus* because that has become so common for referring to a capo at 022200.

The DADGAD tuning itself is quite similar to the *Esus* capo configuration in standard tuning (see page 810) and this configuration of the capo behaves a lot like another common standard tuning configuration where the *Esus* capo is on the 4th fret in standard tuning: 044400. It gives the same additional open strings on the outside, but on the inner strings, things are different.

This situation yields some pretty interesting chord voicings and inversions, though it is not the kind of thing you would do for days on end like some of the "deeper" partial capo configurations. This would be a quick way to get some different sounds, and an environment you might want to work up some music in to help you get a different sound.

Songwriter David Wilcox does this sometimes, and may have originated it.

There are a few good chords that require reaching over the capo, so as you might expect you are probably going to be happier with a *Kyser* or *Shubb Esus* capo (shown) than a universal capo to do this. A *Liberty "Flip"* can do this from either side of the fingerboard in case you want access from one side in particular.

A ***Shubb Esus** (c7b)* capo forming the DADGAD Esus configuration.

"POWER CHORDS"

The "power chord," (sometimes called "*neutral,*" "*modal,*" or "*indeterminate*") chord, because it has 1's and 5's and no musical 3rd) has no official name, and it is technically not even a chord. This chord is widely used in modal music, and electric guitarists love them for crashing rhythm. Power chords offer soloists more options for playing over them, since they do not establish "tonality" the way major or minor chords do. I notate it as E5 in this book, which is the most common symbol used for it in guitar publications. There are only a few ways to play them in standard tuning, and dozens of examples in this book with only 1-5 notes. You might also see a "chord" that is all 1's and 3's, with no 5th that I sometimes call a D3 or an E3 chord, though it is not "officially" a chord either.

0 2 2 2 0 0

Some Chords in the DADGAD Esus Configuration p.1
TUNING: D A D G A D

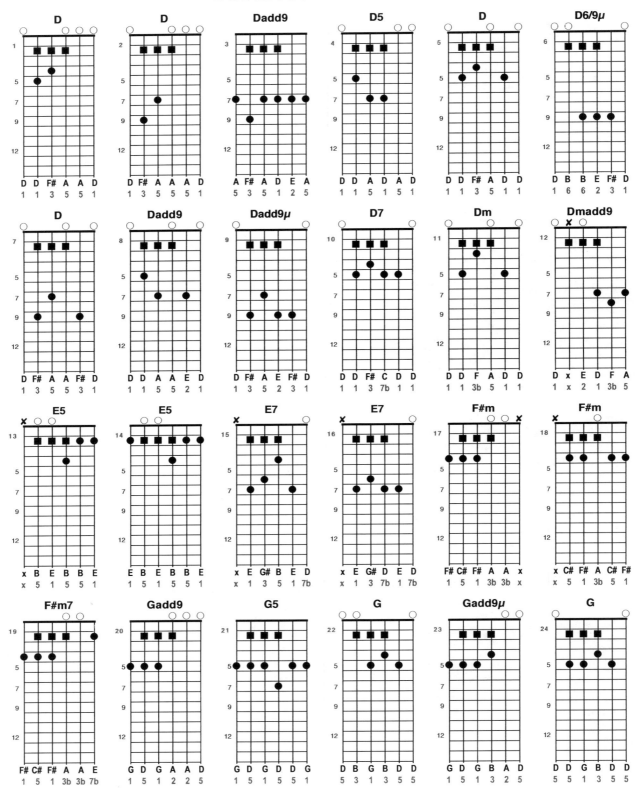

Some Chords in the DADGAD Esus Configuration p.2
TUNING: D A D G A D

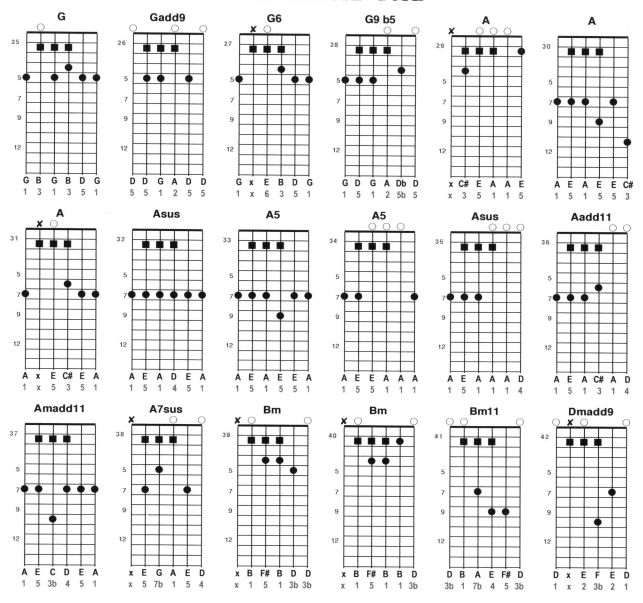

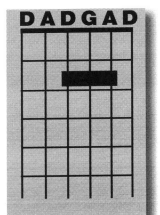

5- "Open A" 002220

This one is a slight variation of the first 0 0 2 2 2 2 configuration, although this time we just leave the high E string open to sound the D note on top. It's easy to do with a common *Esus* 3-string partial capo.

Like the previous *"Esus"* configuration, I have chosen to call it *"Open A"* although the capo does not sound an A chord in DADGAD tuning the way it does in standard. It is a struggle to find names to refer to these configurations, and it helps when you have a nickname you can use that is not just the sequence of capo numbers.

Interestingly, although configuration #1 (002222) worked well for playing in A, this one seems more useful for playing in D. It offers some very nice chords and a more "dreamy" and "extended chord" flavor that is less Celtic sounding than you usually get from DADGAD tuning. It is surprisingly different from the 002222 situation, which at a glance seems very similar.

There are not many chords that require reaching over the capo, so a universal capo can do this fine, as will any of the 3-string *Esus* type capos.

A Liberty "Flip" capo forming the Open A configuration in DADGAD tuning.

CHORD NAME CONFUSION

There is no universal chord-naming system or standard. The names *Esus* and *Esus4* for the *suspended* chord (1-4-5 scale notes) are used interchangeably. Some people (including me) call an added 9th note (scale degree 2) an *"add9"* chord, while some call the same thing an *"add2."* Technically, it has to do with which octave the added note is in, but since guitar chords are always scattered across several octaves, guitarists are often less rigorous, and may call a chord with an added 2nd a 9th. (It could be technically a 16th also, but nobody bothers to do that.)

The *slash chord* notation is sometimes used, especially in guitar books, for a *"Mr. Bojangles"* type descending bass line that is played against a chord. When you play a C chord and "walk" down a bass line underneath, it makes sense to think of the progression as C/C, C/B (C chord with a B bass note), C/A etc. rather than as a chord based on the root note B then one based on A. I support this idea, and have included a few of them in this book. (p.27 chord #11)

0 0 2 2 2 0

Some Chords in the DADGAD "Open A" Configuration p.1
TUNING: D A D G A D

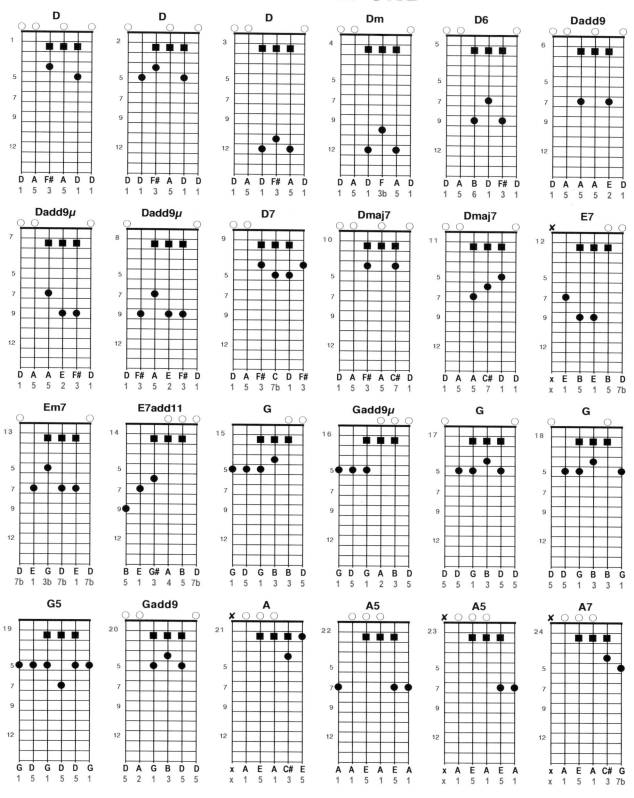

Some Chords in the DADGAD "Open A" Configuration p.2
TUNING: DADGAD

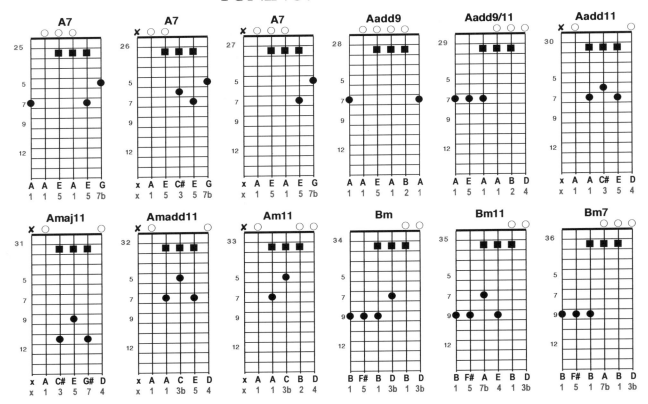

ABOUT ARPEGGIATED CHORDS

I mention often in this book that certain chords work better if you arpeggiate the notes. The word *arpeggio* is Italian for "broken chord," which means you play the note in staggered time rather than all at once. Your ear will often hear two notes played together as dissonant, while if they are separated by time they will sound much less so. Some chords in this book contain 4 or even 5 different scale notes on different strings (this sort of thing is much more common in the world of the partial capo than you usually encounter on guitar) and when arpeggiated they flow like a harp playing melodies. When strummed they can sound dreadful.

On harp or a piano, doing this is a matter of playing the notes in succession rather than all at once. On guitar, success depends on right hand skills. If you play fingerstyle, you have more options, but even with a flat pick, you can either drag down or up across a group of strings, or do some "*sweep picking*" or "*cross picking*" which involves weaving a flatpick up and down among a group of strings quickly in a way that simulates fingerpicking. The dexterity that some players develop is startling. A lot of guitarists (especially on electric guitar and with lighter string gauges) also use a flatpick and their fingers together to play a hybrid fingerpicking style. A few players even use fingerpicks and a flatpick together to solve this problem. So if a chord in this book sounds really odd or dissonant, try arpeggiating it a few different ways up and down before you decide it is not a "good chord."

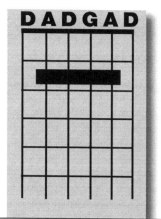

 # 6 – "Middle 4 @2" 022220

This is a pretty typical partial capo situation, where you get a few nice new options and sounds, but there is not a startling new world of possibilities. It is crucial to understand that the partial capo offers as wide a range of new options in each tuning as it does in standard tuning.

The fact that you still have both outer strings sounding the D notes suggests that you might still want to play in keys centered around D. The new bass strings are not typical of open tuning or capo situations, since the bottom 3 strings are the 1-6-9 scale degrees in the key of D.

There are not many chords that require reaching over the capo, so a universal capo can do this fine. Your other option is to use a *Kyser K-Lever RED* or a *Liberty "Flip"* that can both clamp the middle 4 strings.

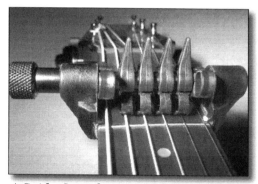

A *SpiderCapo* forming a DADGAD 022220 configuration.

SOMETHING TO THINK ABOUT

If you play a D and a D# simultaneously (or any musical *interval* of a *"minor 2nd"* –which means 2 adjacent keys on the piano) they are quite dissonant. You can hear this on a guitar with no capos at all– in DADGAD tuning, just play the 6th fret of the 2nd string [D#] and the open 1st string [D] at the same time.

Now try separating the notes D-D# by an octave and play them again. (This time play the open 4th string [D] and the 1st fret of the high string [D#]. The result is much less dissonant. If you play the open 6th string [D] and fret 1 of the 1st string [D#] simultaneously and separate the D from the D# by still another octave, the interval of D-D# is no longer dissonant.

What this means for you is that when you capo up very high on the neck, and still drone some open bass strings, the results are often less dissonant than you expect. Sometimes chords and inversions of chords sound fine if they are spread across several octaves, even though the same letter-named notes would not sound as good if they were closer together in overall pitch. For example, there are some #5 and b5 chords in this book, and those normally dissonant notes are sometimes really nice when they are played on the high strings against a root bass note.

0 2 2 2 2 0

Some Chords in the DADGAD "022220" Configuration p.1
TUNING: DADGAD

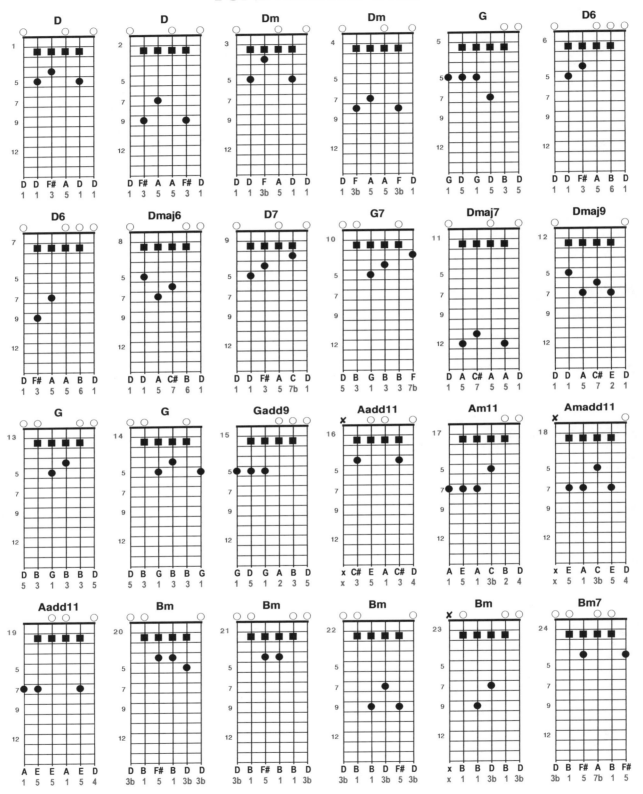

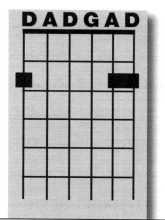

7- "Faux-Standard" 200022

This is a good example of how confusing partial capos can be, especially when combined with a tuning. To a partial capo novice or a non-guitarist, this should behave much like standard tuning, since the capo here is "reversing" the lowered strings that makes DADGAD from standard, and makes the open strings the same as in standard tuning.

Since the guitar is still in DADGAD, it does not feel like standard tuning at all, and nothing you would normally play in standard works at all. Don't try to fingerpick *"Freight Train!"* Chords and scales all have nothing to do with standard tuning shapes or sounds.

There are a few chords, however, particularly in the key of A, that sound like "normal" standard-tuning chord voicings rather than an open tuning. The A-E7 chord change (chords #8 and #21) is a good example of this. You have some nice D chords, as you might expect from being in DADGAD, but the low D string being capoed to E prevents the big D chord sound you are expecting in this tuning.

You can get a few G root chords (I include one full G chord,) and quite a few E, E7, Em7 and other extensions based on the E root. Your best bets here are to play in E or A.

The only option for this configuration is to use a universal capo.

A *Third Hand* capo forming a DADGAD 200022 "Faux-Standard" configuration.

PARTIAL CAPOS AND INTONATION

Intonation is the word for the ability of an instrument (or a singer or player of variable pitch instruments like violins and horns) to play correct musical pitches. The theory and science of musical pitch, the definition of what it means to be "in tune," and the skill and craftsmanship involved in making instruments are all surprisingly complicated, yet worth mentioning here. Not all guitars are capable of playing "in tune." The shape, size and placement of the bridge, nut, frets and saddle combine with the neck shape, bow and angle to create a very complex system that few really understand. It is probably a fact also that in recent decades, guitar manufacturing has become a more precise operation, and modern guitars generally play in tune better than old ones. The ***compensated saddle*** has probably done more than anything to improve guitar intonation. On most guitars now, the saddle is not straight, and the 6 strings are not exactly the same length. The B and G strings are often slightly different.

A big reason why partial capoing has become much more popular in recent years is probably that it challenges the intonation of a guitar. Older guitars might not have been able to produce proper notes with capos all over the neck, and people may have tried the idea in the past and not liked what they heard.

200022

Some Chords in the "Faux-Standard" 200022 Configuration p.1
TUNING: D A D G A D

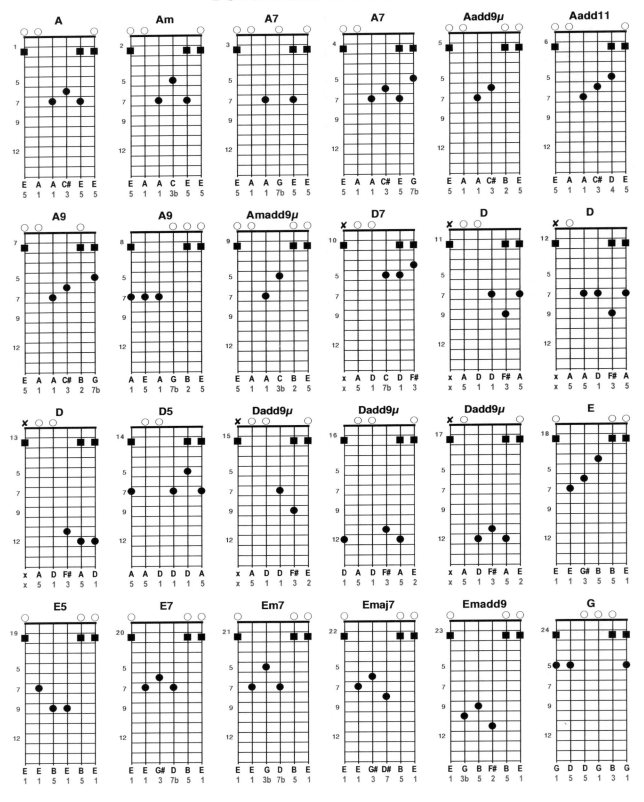

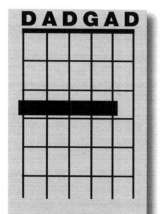

8- "Bottom 5 @3" 333330

You might notice that I did not include 222220 or 022222, which are the most basic partial capo configurations in standard tuning. The first of those just adds a flat 7 on the open top string, which adds a D note to an E chord. Though it might be just what you need, I found it somehow contrary to the "spirit" of the DADGAD tuning. The other provides a bass D note, which would suggest playing in C above the capo to sound in D-- not a great use of this tuning either.

Moving the capo up to fret 3, which is an odd thing to do in standard tuning, causes a lot of good things happen in this tuning. The key center shifts to F, and you get the top 3 open strings sounding the 4-5-6 notes of the scale. Certain inversions like chord #4 have 3-4-5-6 scale notes all in a row and when arpeggiated, especially in reverse order or with the fingers while the thumb hits the bass string, make a stunning chord. You also have the 1-4 chord change all in 9ths with chords #18 and #27-29 that make a jazzy blues sound, and you have chords #24-37 that you can use for your 5 (C) chords to complete a 3-chord blues progression. You even have some excellent 2 chords (G7, Gm7 etc.) You may notice a lot of add9μ and minor add9μ chords, which happens more often in partial capo situations than in standard tuning, though there are a number of them that are available in DADGAD tuning.

With this configuration you can jump from a DADGAD tuning in D to a "swingy" blues in F with just an offset capo.

There are no chords shown here that require reaching over the capo, so a universal capo can do this fine, as can all the 5-string shortened capos like the *Shubb c8b*, *Kyser Drop D*, *G7 Newport*, or an offset full capo (see photo.)

A Shubb c1b full capo offset to form the DADGAD 333330 configuration.

SO MANY CHOICES FOR CHORDS

It's hard to wrap your mind around the fact that there can be so many ways to voice the same chord, and that they have different musical value. You may only be aware of a few different ways to play a chord, and not realize that there can be so many choices. This is a vital reason why we use both tunings and partial capos-- not just to get open string resonances, but to be able to get a whole new "menu" of choices for our chords, with different "flavors" and "moods."

There are some distinctive and really noticeable voicings in this book that might be just what you want for writing or arranging a song, and the ones you like will depend on the song. New voicings can add a whole new dimension to your music. It's also not intuitive that so many of the chord voicings in this book are unique, and appear only once.

Using an open tuning or a partial capo really brings this all into focus. You also have this same "diversity" of voicings when you use an open tuning, but since the names of the notes on the fingerboard all change whenever you change the tuning, it's not as easy to be aware of what is going on. In the chord diagrams in this book I show you where every note lies in every chord. It's a great theory lesson to study the small numbers below each chord.

333330

Some Chords in the DADGAD "333330" Configuration p.1
TUNING: D A D G A D

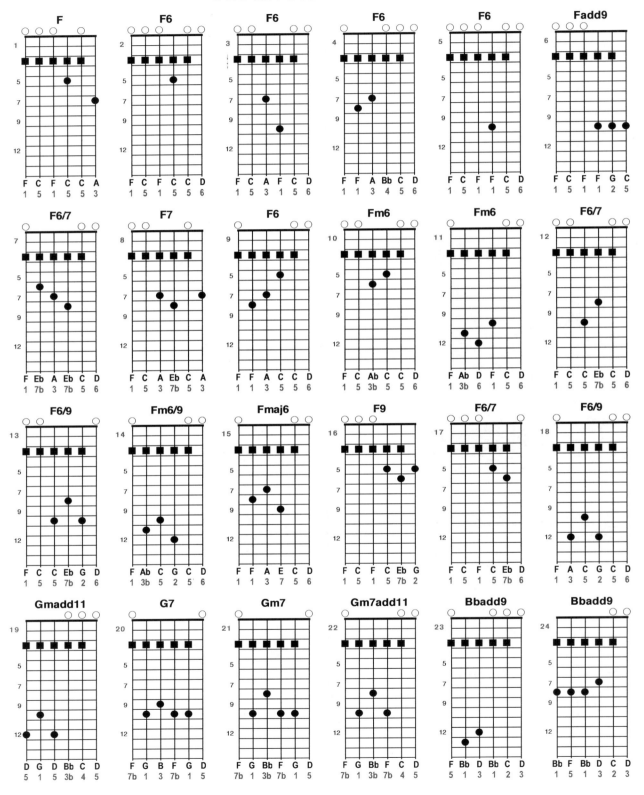

Some Chords in the DADGAD "333330" Configuration p.2
TUNING: DADGAD

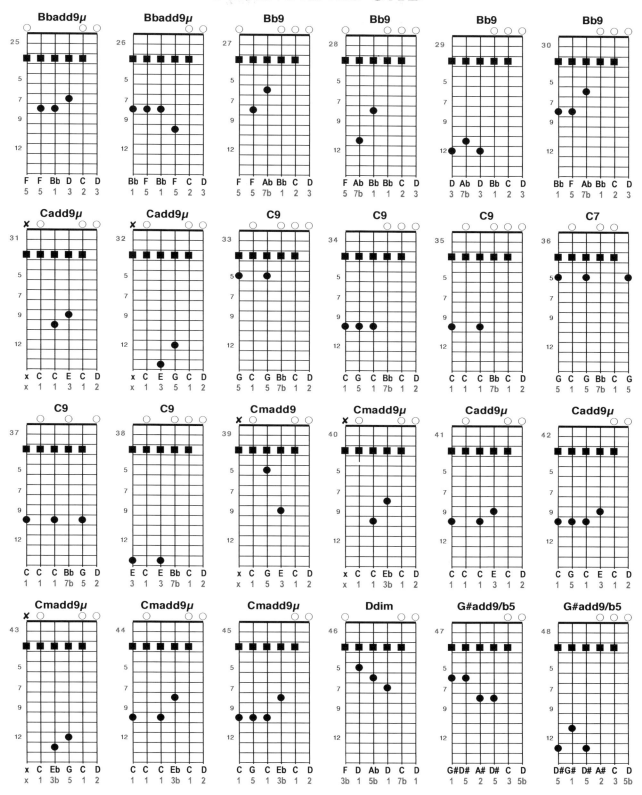

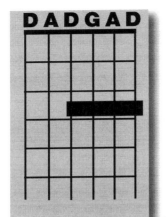

9 – "Top 4 @3" 003333

There is quite a family of useful configurations here at fret 3 in this tuning. With the bottom two strings open, we get another group of possibilities. This one was brought to my attention by Canadian guitarist Phil Schappert.

The best results with this are in D minor or D *Dorian*, since the bottom 3 strings form a Dm triad with the 1-3b-5 notes.

To effectively play in these keys, you need either a C major or an A chord, and preferably both. There are a number of partial capo environments that provide one or the other, but they both work here. You also get the F, G Bb and Gm chords that commonly occur in these keys, so you would have a good chance of working up arrangements of well-known minor-key songs in this set-up, as well as inventing new music.

There are no chords shown here that require reaching over the capo, so a universal capo can do this fine, as can the *Planet Waves Trio* on most guitars, and probably a *Liberty "Flip."* The 5-string shortened capos like the *Shubb c8b, Kyser Drop D* or an offset full capo likely will not work properly.

A Planet Waves Trio offset to form the DADGAD 003333 configuration.

0 0 3 3 3 3

Some Chords in the DADGAD "003333" Configuration p.1
TUNING: D A D G A D

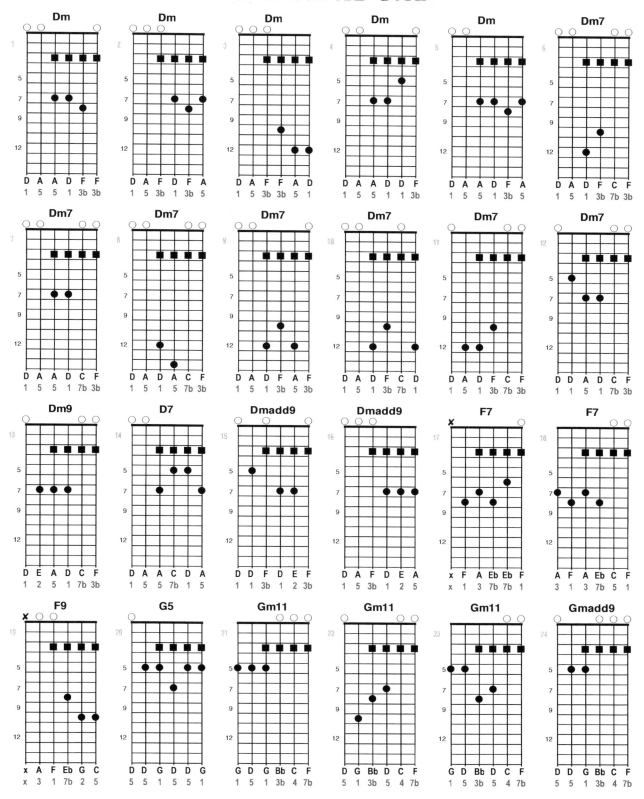

Some Chords in the DADGAD "003333" Configuration p.2
TUNING: DADGAD

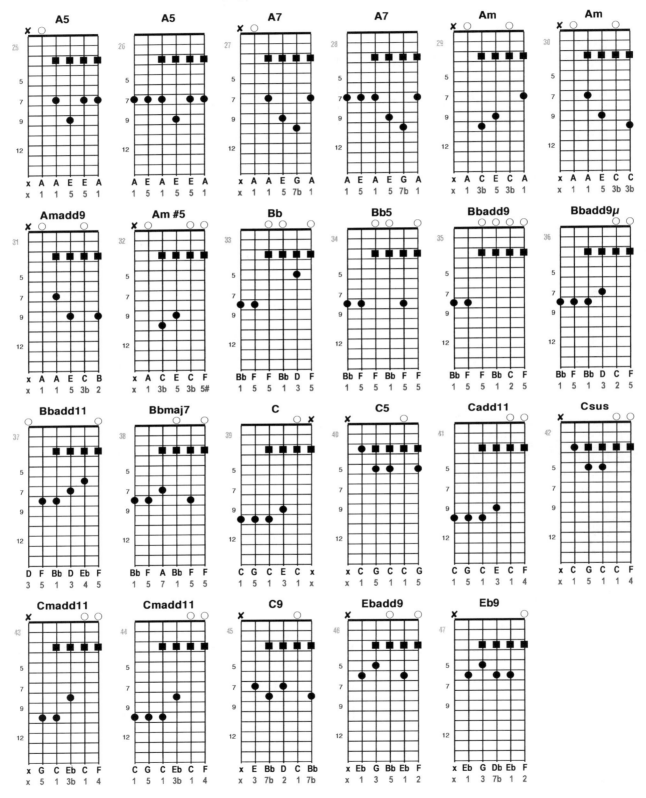

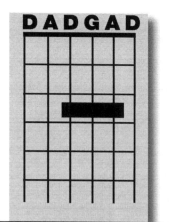

 # 10- "Open A @3" 003330

Since this one has a D minor triad on the bottom 3 open strings, it makes sense to use it for playing in Dm or D *Dorian* mode. There are some nice extensions of Gm and a number of Bb chords. The key of Gm is closely related to B♭, and you can play some things centered there also.

It is hard to play any chords that are not extended, and there are some really nice 9ths and 6ths, that all pull you away from the more common Celtic flavor of the tuning.

This is the kind of environment where you might want to create some music, rather than arranging well-known melodies. There are some nice but unusual chords here, and a lot of things that don't work easily. Because it is not clear what the best key center is for this, I have put the chords in alphabetical order in the charts on the next 2 pages.

There are not many chords that require reaching over the capo, so a universal capo can do this fine, as will any of the 3-string *Esus* type capos. Otherwise you can use an *Esus* or *Liberty "Flip" Model 43* capo.

A *Kyser Short-Cut* capo forming DADGAD 003330 configuration.

PARTIAL CAPOS & 12-STRING GUITARS

12-string players are used to having their own set of problems, and everything from strings, cases, capos, pickups are often a little different than on 6-string. The partial capo has huge value for 12-string players, especially the modern breed of them who were inspired by the roaring open-tuned sound of Leo Kottke.

You can get the same kind of huge sound with a partial capo, and there is less retuning than if you use actual tuning changes. Since the fingerboards are usually wider, you have fewer hardware choices for partial capos. The *SpiderCapo* mechanism does not work with pairs of strings, and the *G-Band* may not either. The standard *Esus* capos will probably work at the 2nd fret, but will most likely not be long enough to work at higher frets. (You need to shorten a *Shubb c8b*.) You may also have trouble with the octave A string buzzing. With a *Third Hand* capo, you can spread the discs apart to accommodate any string spacing, as well as shave or notch the rubber cam disc slightly where the bass A string hits it, to allow more rubber to contact the octave string.

Your best strategy is to experiment with a *Third Hand*, and once you settle on some favorite configurations, you might want to make some single-purpose capos, especially if you are a performer.

0 0 3 3 3 0

Some Chords in the DADGAD "003330" Configuration p.1
TUNING: DADGAD

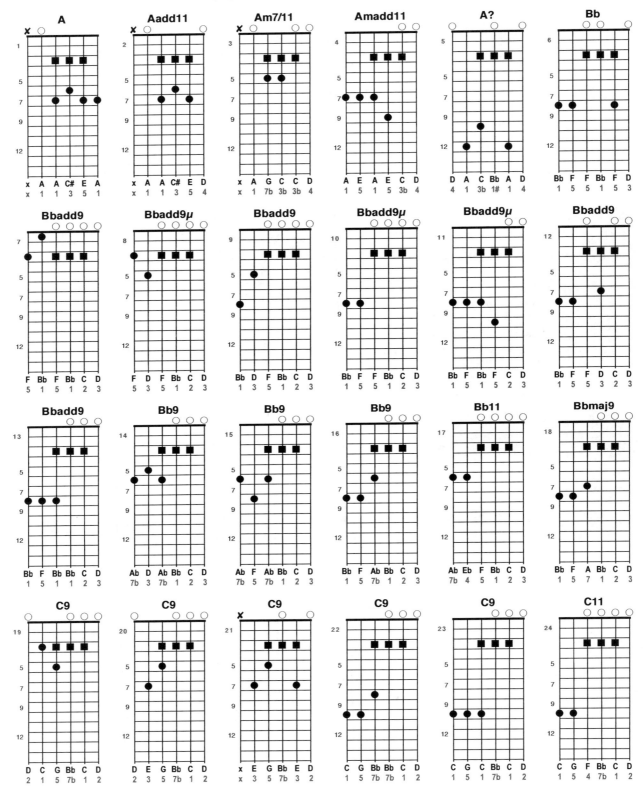

Some Chords in the DADGAD "003330" Configuration p.2
TUNING: DADGAD

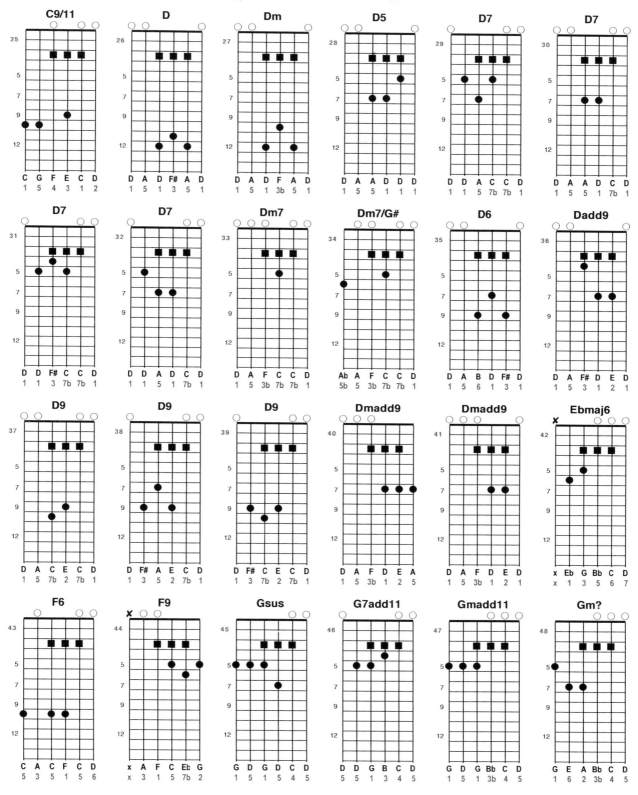

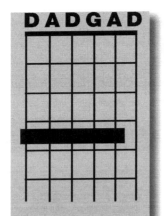

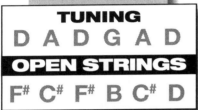

11 – "Bottom 5 @4" 444440

This one is pretty simple, since it just adds the D note on top of a lot of things, and there are no complicated inner voicings going on. This is the kind of thing you can easily do, easily adapt to, and it is the kind of partial capo environment you would likely use for a few songs to add some variety to your sound in this tuning.

It is inevitable that once players start exploring the use of partial capos with the huge number of tunings already in use, a similarly large number of new partial capo ideas like this one will surface. It will take a long time to sift through them all to find the ones that are really useful. A lot of partial capo configurations are only slightly useful, though that judgment is quite subjective, since there are a lot of kinds of music out there. There are literally hundreds of guitar tunings in use, and many kinds of partial capos, so the number of possible combinations of tunings and capos is almost overwhelmingly large.

Because this one starts in D and has a capo 4, it will yield a lot of music in $F^\#$, which is both an advantage and a disadvantage depending how you look at it. There is no musical reason that $F^\#$ is so rarely used, except that in the world of written music it is clumsy, and few instruments can play in this key without effort. For singers or listeners, it is as good as any other key, and it can't hurt to use it now and then, especially if you tend to avoid it.

The very close musical distance between the top 3 strings here means that cascading, harp-like sounds will be readily available. Arpeggiating or fingerpicking the treble side of the guitar while moving lines around on the bass side is probably the best approach to this situation, though you might enjoy the dissonance of strumming the B-$C^\#$-D notes together also.

There are not many chords that require reaching over the capo, so a universal capo can do this fine, as will any number of full and shortened capos.

A Shubb c8b capo forming a "DADGAD Bottom 5 @4" 444440 configuration.

Don't forget that you can always put on a full capo below one or more partial capos. It just raises the pitch of everything. You'll need to do this for singing in certain keys, playing along with other instruments, or just to get a brighter and different timbre from your guitar.

444440

Some Chords in the DADGAD 4 4 4 4 4 0 Configuration p.1
TUNING: D A D G A D

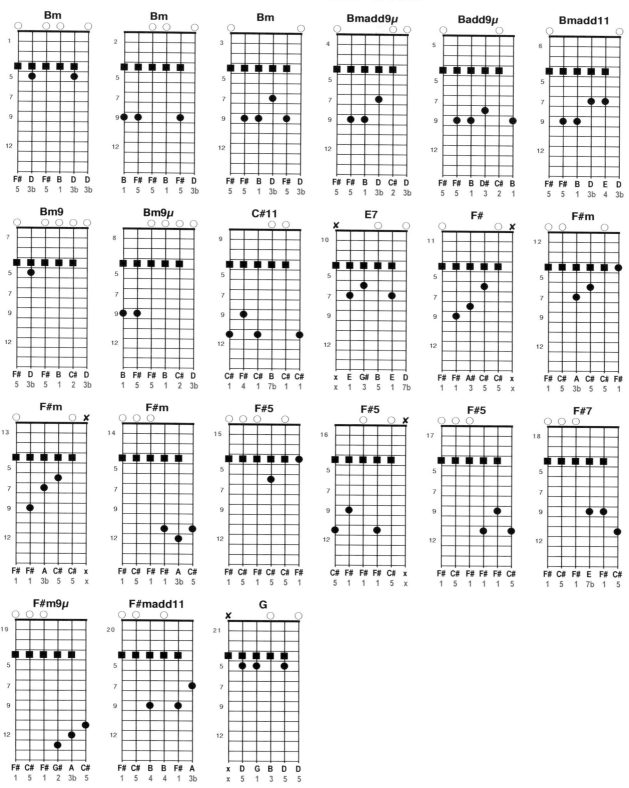

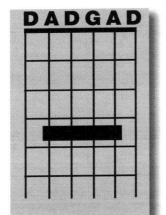

12- "Middle 4 @4" 044440

Only the bass string is different from the previous 444440 configuration, but it makes it a very different environment. The presence of the bass D string means that it is not a great idea to play in F# like the previous one, and the logical thing to do is to see what happens when you play in D.

The capo adds some interesting notes: the middle 4 strings clamped by the capo are the 3rd, 6th and major 7th of the D scale. This suggests using Dmaj7 chords, and looking in the Bm family, and there are several great voicings of those. The fact that the top 3 strings create a B-C#-D sequence, which is the last 6-7-8 notes of the D scale, means that arpeggiated chords will be readily available and probably sound better than strumming.

You can actually play things in both D and A, and I think I like A more. Because this is a situation that generates some very unusual chord voicings, it is the kind of configuration you would probably use to create a song or two to add some contrast to whatever else you are doing in this tuning.

Several of the chord voicings are completely unique, and are the only times I have encountered their particular spellings among the nearly 10000 partial capo chords I have assembled for my research.

There are not many chords that require reaching over the capo, so a universal capo can do this fine, or a *Liberty "Flip"*.

A *Liberty "Flip"* Model 43 forming a DADGAD 044440 configuration.

INVERSIONS & DOUBLING

I use some terms from music theory that I should define a little better. The *voicing* of a group of notes is a description of which notes appear in what order. Chord names usually don't mention the notes that are *omitted*, and these affect the sound. (Piano theory people are generally more strict about terminology than in guitar.) Since guitar only has a few strings, to play complex jazz chords there are usually notes omitted. With 6 guitar strings, and only three or four notes in many chords, there are typically repeated or *doubled* notes. The word *inversion* is used to describe the order the notes appear in. Technically, a *1st inversion* major triad has the 3rd in the bass, and a *2nd inversion* has the 5th in the bass. It makes a huge difference in the sound of a chord which is the lowest note, and generally chords sound odd if there is anything but a 1 or 5 on the bottom. Of course, there are musical uses for the various inversions of chords, and sometimes an unusual chord voicing or inversion is at the heart of a famous version of a song. Adding 7ths 9ths, 11ths, 13th etc. onto basic chords are usually called *extensions*, and partial capos really change the opportunities of what inversions and voicings of many kinds of chords can be played on guitar.

0 4 4 4 4 0

Some Chords in the DADGAD 0 4 4 4 4 0 Configuration p.1
TUNING: DADGAD

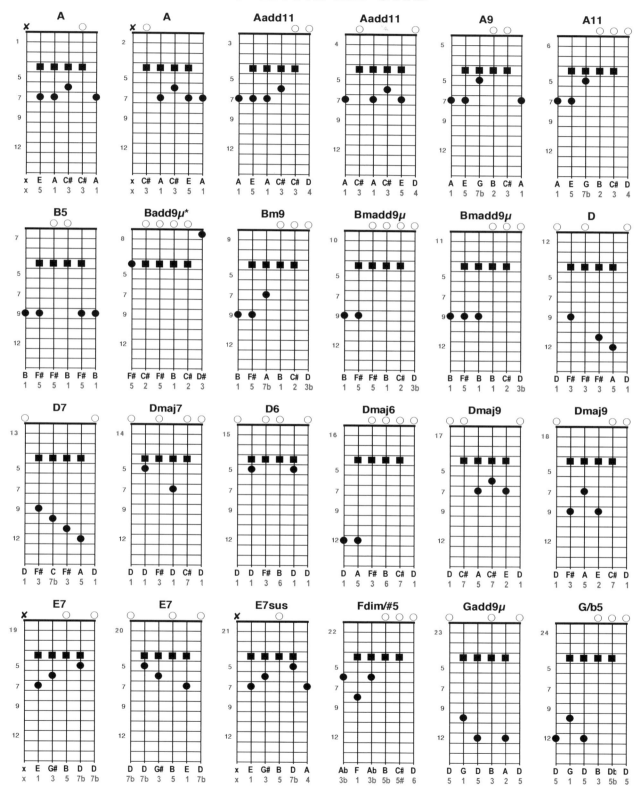

13- "Middle 2 @4" 004400

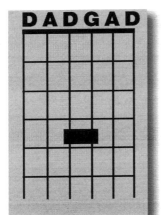

TUNING: DADGAD
OPEN STRINGS: D A F# B A D

You get the best sounds from this one by still playing in D, since you still have the bass D and A strings. There are some nice and more complex extensions to the chords that sound really good when they are arpeggiated. With the F# and B open strings, which are the 2 and 6 scale degrees in D, it makes a few nice new chords available. This is not a revelation or a rich partial capo environment, but it has some good sounds. It is also another example of an uncommon way to use the capos, since there are no common partial capo configurations that only clamp 2 inner strings.

There are a few good chords that require reaching over the capo, but basically a universal capo can do this fine. The 2-string capo shown in the photo can be a bit unstable, but it does allow much more access to the surrounding fingerboard, and might well be worth the risk of having it move around a little if you bump it.

*A sawed-off **Shubb c7b** capo at the 4th fret making the DADGAD 004400 configuration.*

MORE CHORD NAME THOUGHTS

There is no real standardization of the process of naming guitar chords, and there remain a lot of "gray areas." In classical music, there really is not a tradition of naming all chords, and only a few special ones like the *Neapolitan* chord have been given names. In the worlds of folk, jazz and rock, people often do different things. I encourage everyone to relax about it all. The conventions people use are like dialects of language, and they even change with time. I speak more the folk and rock guitar here.

This is the only guitar book I know of that actually shows the note names and scale positions of every note in every chord. So even if you don't like or understand the names I use, you can still study the structure.

004400

Some Chords in the DADGAD "004400" Configuration p.1
TUNING: DADGAD

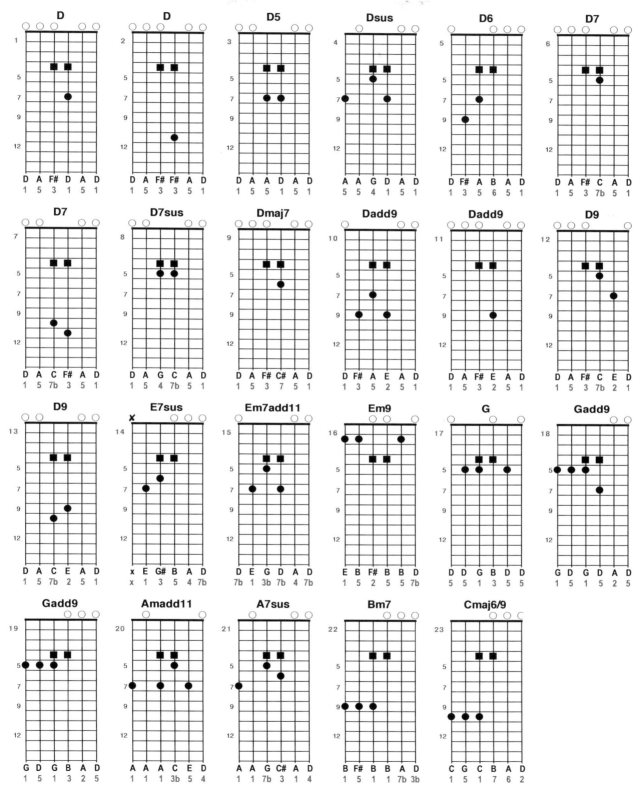

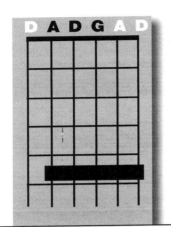

14- 055555 [DADGAD]

I skipped this one when I first published my DADGAD partial capo book, since I did not think it offered much, especially as compared to what some other configurations can provide. But I have heard from several people who use it, and thought it might be instructive to include it. The low D string ringing in an environment that is essentially set up to play in G gives a big bass sound on your 5 chord in that key. When you play anything else, it is a distraction, and it gets in the way when you try to play essentially anything but a D or G chord. This means you need to mute it or fret it above the capo pretty much all the time, which you will see happening in the chords here.

If you have never used a partial capo before, this might seem to be useful because it does change the landscape a little, and when you play a 5 chord in G (which "feels" like an A) you no longer have to mute the bass string. Usually in DADGAD you can only use the bass string in a 1 or a 4 chord, and now you "trade" that for the ability to use it in a 1 and 5 situation, which does have some value.

A Planet Waves Dual-Action in DADGAD tuning at fret 5.

055555

Some Chords in the DADGAD 055555 Configuration p.1
TUNING: DADGAD

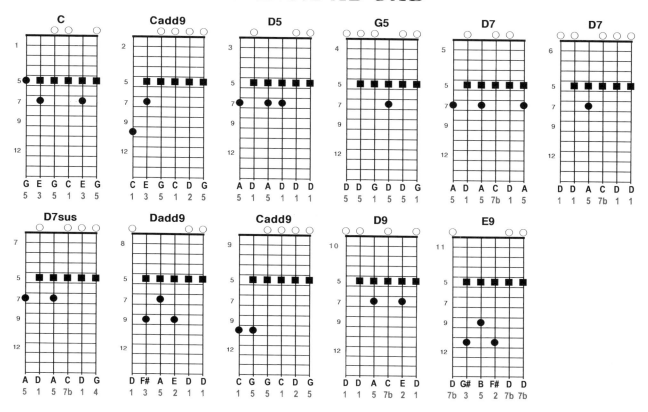

47

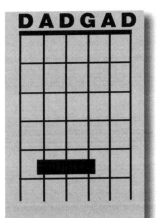

15- "Esus @5" 055500

You get the best sounds from this one still playing in D, though there are some more complex extensions to the chords that sound really good when they are arpeggiated.

Not all partial capo configurations are equally useful, and "less fruitful" capo environments like this are worth experimenting with, since they help you better understand how partial capos work and don't work. It also helps you appreciate the ones that work better. There is a perpetual mystery about it all, and after 35 years of using partial capos, I still can't be sure what is going to happen until I dive in and start trying to play music with a capo somewhere new.

There are a few good chords that require reaching over the capo, so although a universal capo can do this fine, you'll be happiest with any of the 3-string *Esus* type capos or a *Liberty "Flip"*.

A *Kyser "Short-Cut"* capo at the 5th fret making the DADGAD 055500 configuration.

ABOUT CHORD SHAPES

Because of the nature of music and of the guitar, it often turns out that a chord you find in this book (or one you find on your own) can be moved up or down the fingerboard, or even across, to generate something musical.

If you find a chord you like here, even if it has a lot of open strings and is not technically a "movable" chord, try moving it up or down 2 frets and see what it sounds like when you switch between the two similar shapes. You can often also move a shape up 4, 5 or 7 frets and find a musically compatible chord.

Especially on the bass side of the guitar, you can sometimes move a shape "sideways" one string, either higher or lower, and find good sounds. Your ear is your guide. A lot of songs have been written and arranged using these kinds of "germs." Feel free to move chords shapes around like this. I have included a lot of these kinds of "matching pairs" in this book, and their names often offer no clues that they are musically related. Look for similar shapes in these pages of chords and play them in succession to see what you can find. Many great songs have started this way.

0 5 5 5 0 0

Some Chords in the DADGAD "055500" Configuration p.1
TUNING: DADGAD

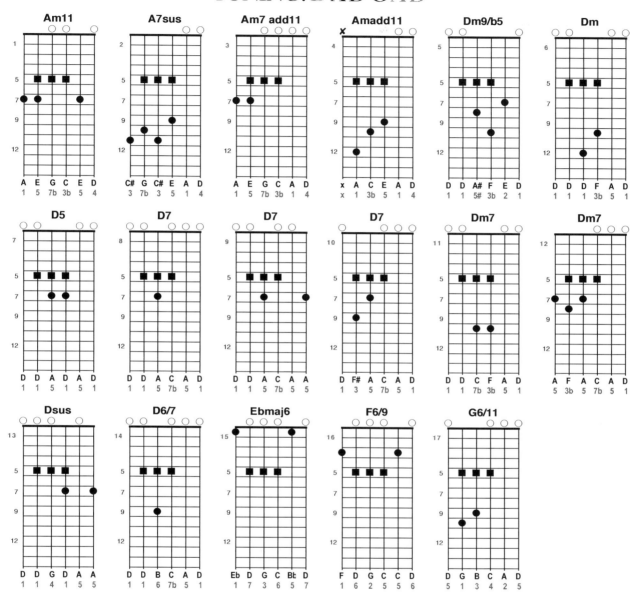

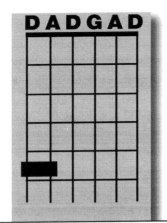

 # 16~ "Bottom 2 @5" 550000

Here we get another new set of musical options that are extra surprising to users of tunings who frequently don't also use partial capos.

Since we have capoed the two bass strings up a fourth, with a G on the bottom end now, it makes sense that this is a way to play music in keys associated with G, including G major, G minor and modal keys rooted in G. If you look at the chords #1-8 you see a number of G and modal G5 tonic (1) chords, and also chords #9-22 give you a wealth of Gm family chords. You might also notice that because you have an open A note on your 2nd string, this adds a 9th to the G and Gm chords, and almost always in the *"mu"* form. (See p.14) This means that both the 2nd and the 3rd or flat 3rd are both present in the same octave, which is an effect common in partial capoing, but not otherwise easy to obtain on guitar. They tend to sound best when arpeggiated.

The only really good way to do this is with a *Woodie's G-Band Model 2* capo. You may have some trouble getting it to stay in place, depending on your string gauge, action and neck profile. Presumably you have a universal capo, and like is often the case, you can experiment with it and get a sense of how much you like it, and then decide if it is worth getting a single-purpose capo to do the job.

*A **Woodie's G-Band Model 2** making a 550000 configuration.*

550000

Some Chords in the DADGAD 550000 Configuration p.1
TUNING: DADGAD

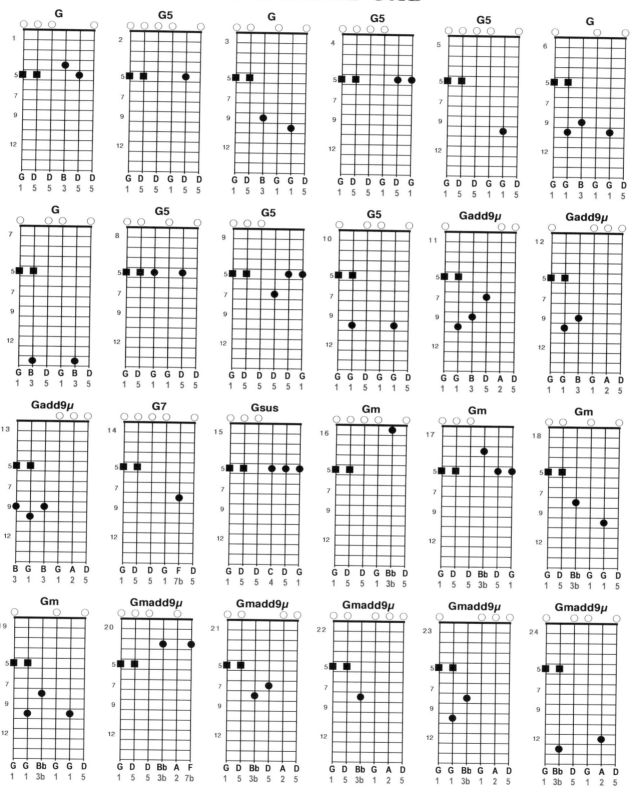

Some Chords in the DADGAD 550000 Configuration p.2
TUNING: D A D G A D

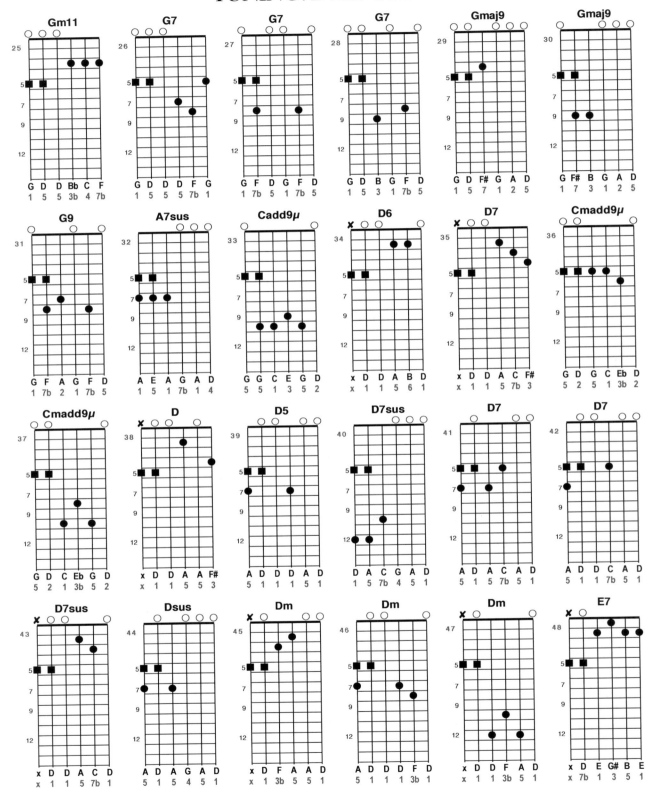

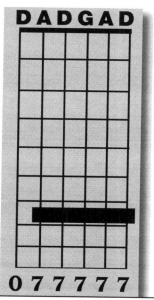

17~ "Top 5 @7" 077777

If you don't have a 14-fret neck or a cutaway this one could be hard to manage, since the capo ties up quite a bit of the fretboard.

This is not a rich environment of possibilities, but there are some sweet voicings of chords, and it would be worth using this one just for playing some fingerpicked 1-4-5 songs in D using chords 1, 7 and 16 as your 3 basic chords. They go very well together and they have a distinctive and fresh, yet familiar sound.

You can easily do this by offsetting a normal capo, or with the Liberty 65, *Shubb c8b,* **Planet Waves "Trio,"** *Kyser* **"Drop D,"** *G7* **Newport or as always, a universal capo.**

*A **Liberty "Flip"** Model 65 capo at the 7th fret making the "DADGAD 777700" configuration.*

077777

Some Chords in the DADGAD "077777" Configuration p.1
TUNING: DADGAD

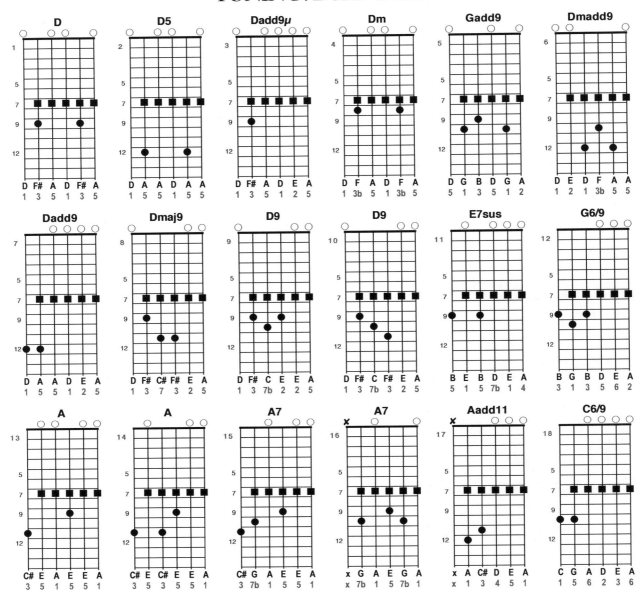

18~"Top 4 @7" 007777

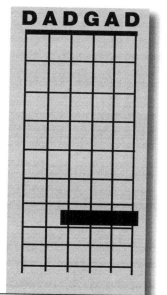

This is not hugely different from the previous one, but the 5th string is open, and as we keep learning: one more bass string ringing can make a huge difference in a solo guitar situation. Partial capo environments like this one that leave some low bass strings ringing along with high treble melody always sound good.

Playing in G position puts you in real D, which means you can leave both bass strings open for the 1 chord, and the 6th string open for the 4 chord (feels like a Cadd9, which you can do now that you have a bass note under it.) You also get a 5 chord in that key by playing what feels like a D chord, though you'll want to mute the bass string or else use chord #6 that adds the 11th fret C# on the bass string. You get a nice one-finger D (chord #17) and some Dadd9 chords (chords #8,9,13) that work as 1 chords and that have a great sound due to the low D string. I can even fingerpick the fiddle tune *"St. Anne's Reel"* if I use chord #18 for the Em (2) chord.

Playing in D or Dm position puts you in A or Am, and your bass root note is now the 5th string. The bass D note is not part of that chord, and you need to again add the 11th fret C# on the bass string (chord #6) for your 1 chord or else skip that string. The low D ringing below it is kind of nice, especially when you play in *Mixolydian* mode, which means using the scale and chords from what feels like G. You don't have a good 5 chord (E) in this key, because the 5th string that usually provides it is now sounding the A, which does not sound great below an E chord, and neither does the bass D string.

The most reliable way to capo just 4 strings is with a Liberty "Flip" Model 43, a *Planet Waves "Trio"* or a universal capo. There are a number of chords and scales where it is helpful to reach over the capo, so a universal capo would not be nearly as useful here.

A **Third Hand** capo at the 7th fret making the 007777 configuration.

007777

Some Chords in the DADGAD 0 0 7777 Configuration p.1
TUNING: DADGAD

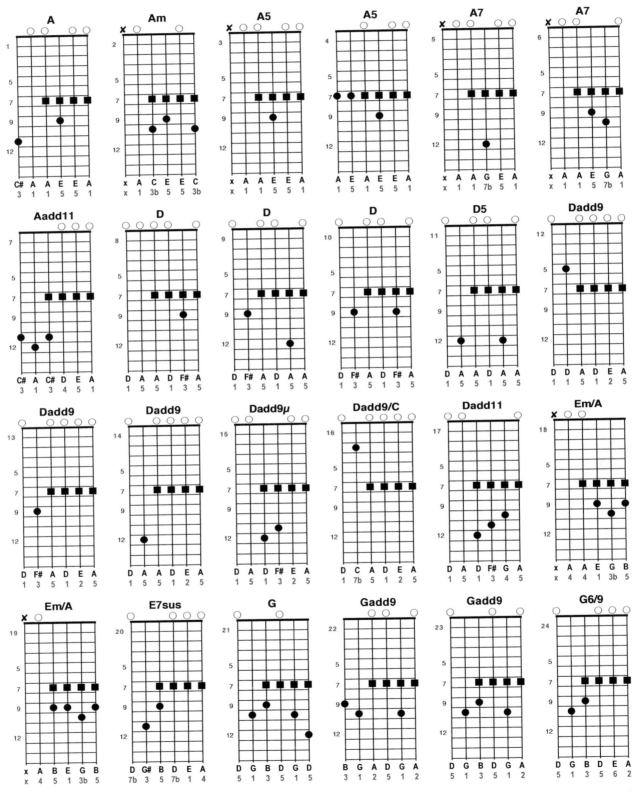

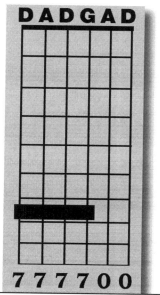

 # 19–"Bottom 4 @7" 777700

DADGAD tuning, as well as some other tunings and capo configurations, yields a lot of music when the open strings form a suspended chord. You'll notice that the open strings here create an *Asus* chord.

This does 4 things for you: It puts you in the key of A, it changes the timbre of the guitar from the low sound of the DADGAD tuning to an airier, brighter one; it gives you some sneaky harp-like open-string scale options on the treble strings; and it also offers a new batch of the close-voiced *"mu"* chords where you have the 2-3, 3 and 4 or 5 and 6 of the scales sounding on adjacent strings in the same octave.

This is helpful, because, like any tuning, the longer you stay in that tuning, the more you are at risk of sounding monotonous. You could play some things in "regular" DADGAD, then do this, and then you can go back to DADGAD and it will sound fresh again.

Because DADGAD has a string "spelling" of 1-5-1 on the bottom three strings, you can play some 2 and 2m chords (in this case, B and Bm family) and have a nice low end for the chords. 2 chords are not often readily available in the world of partial capoing, and it's nice to be able to use them, since they are musically important.

The surest way to do it is with the *Liberty "Flip" Model 43*, *Planet Waves Trio* or *Dual-Action*. You can use a universal capo, but there are some nice chords that require notes beside and behind the capo. You might be able to do this on some guitars by just offsetting a straight capo. You could try doing it with a *Shubb c8b*, *G7 Newport* or *Kyser Drop D* capo that is designed for 5 strings. A *Liberty "Flip"* will probably work fine.

A *Planet Waves Trio* capo at the 7th fret making the DADGAD 777700 configuration.

777700

Some Chords in the DADGAD 7 7 7 7 0 0 Configuration p.1
TUNING: DADGAD

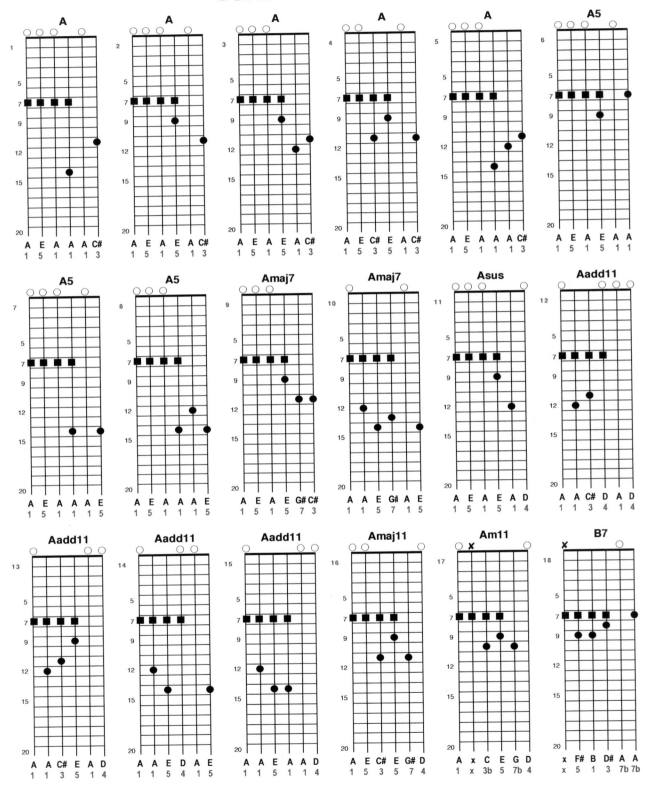

Some Chords in the DADGAD 777700 Configuration p.2
TUNING: DADGAD

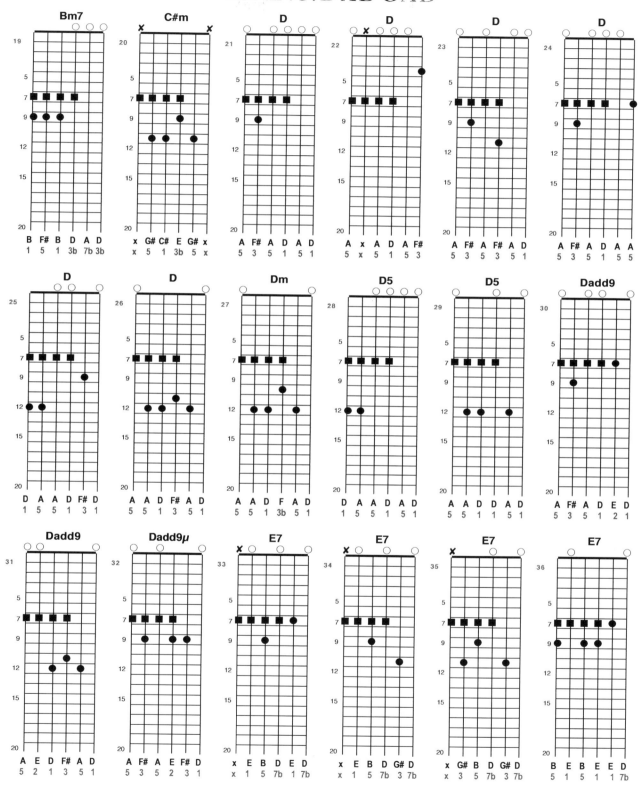

Some Chords in the DADGAD 777700 Configuration p.3
TUNING: DADGAD

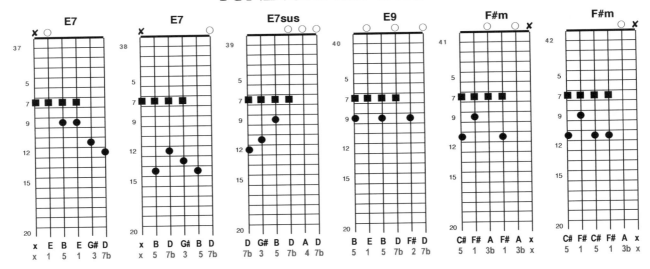

PARTIAL CAPOS, NOTATION & TRANSPOSING

For centuries, guitarists have used capos to change the key, or transpose, as well as to change the tone. This book assumes that you know how to use a regular capo, and if you are rusty, you'll get a lot of practice here keeping track of what key you are in. All the chords in this book are written as they sound. All the notes will show at the bottom of the chord diagram the way they actually sound, with the correct notes. This is not hard to keep track of things when you have a single capo at the 2nd fret in standard tuning, but when there are 2 capos at the 5th and 7th frets and you are playing in a non-standard tuning, it's pretty difficult to stay oriented.

One of the most confusing things about partial capo education is that you always have to say things like "Play what feels like a G chord, and it will sound as an A." That is exactly what you do in a lot of instances, but the language gets thick when you describe things constantly this way.

The problems of partial capo books will get thornier as more people transcribe more arrangements into musical notation. Guitar music is usually written on the staff in standard notation, and when more of it gets arranged and written with partial capos, it will not be totally clear what to do. If you write the music the way it "feels" to a guitarist who knows how to sight-read music, it will not "look like it sounds." When I wrote my guitar books for partial capo, I wrote them in both TAB and standard notation, with TAB (tablature) numbers to show the notes the way they "feel" (with the capo as the 0, and occasional negative numbers for occasional TAB below the capo.) I made the standard notation, however, look the way it sounds, so that a guitarist who knows how to sight-read would not be able to play it as it was written. Computer software for guitar notation does not know about partial capos yet, and people are using several different methods now, including counting from the capo as 0, or counting everything from the nut. It's a thorny issue that is showing no signs of fixing itself.

Since this book is all about using partial capo in non-standard tunings, the notation problem won't come up, since guitarists only use standard notation in standard tuning. Once the MIDI guitars finally get widespread it might be possible to play things in any tuning, and have the computer write out the standard notation as if you were playing in standard tuning. Let's hope they eventually get the accompanying software smart enough to accommodate partial capos, because there will be more and more partial capos on guitars as time passes.

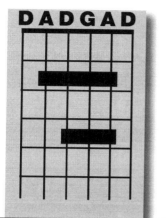

20- 024440

DADGAD tuning allows a lot of close-voiced chords already, since the treble strings are musically much closer to each other than in standard tuning. This configuration is an extreme version of this, since the top 3 strings are only 1 scale step apart musically.

This means that many chords will sound best when arpeggiated, and you will see a lot of the so-called μ or "*mu*" chords (page 14) that have the added 2 along with the 1 and 3 notes. Since there is a bass B note and because the bottom 3 open strings form a B minor triad, the best-sounding things you can do here involve playing in the key of B minor or its related modal keys. The treble strings then add a "*minor add9 μ*" effect, and with some movement in the bass strings against this arpeggiated trio of B-C#-D notes it can be pretty striking. You can just move around on the bass E string and leave everything else droning and it sounds good, since the 6 open strings form a *B minor add 9 μ* chord.

There are not many chords that require reaching over the capo, so a universal capo can work fine as the lower capo, and any of the 3-string *Esus* or *Liberty "Flip"* capos will work there also, as well on the 4th fret. The other option is to use a *Kyser K-Lever RED, BLUE or WHITE* capo for the lower capo, but they are expensive and there really isn't anything you can do to take advantage of the lever, due to the 4th fret capo being in the way of your hand. You could use a *K-Lever BLUE or WHITE* capo at fret 4 and pick up a few new options.

Shubb c7b and *Kyser Short-Cut* capos forming the 0 2 4 4 4 0 configuration. Below: 2 *Kyser K-Lever* capos doing the same thing.

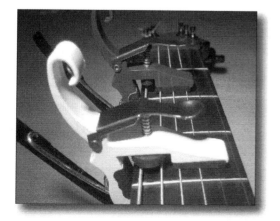

024440

Some Chords in the DADGAD "024440" Configuration p.1
TUNING: DADGAD

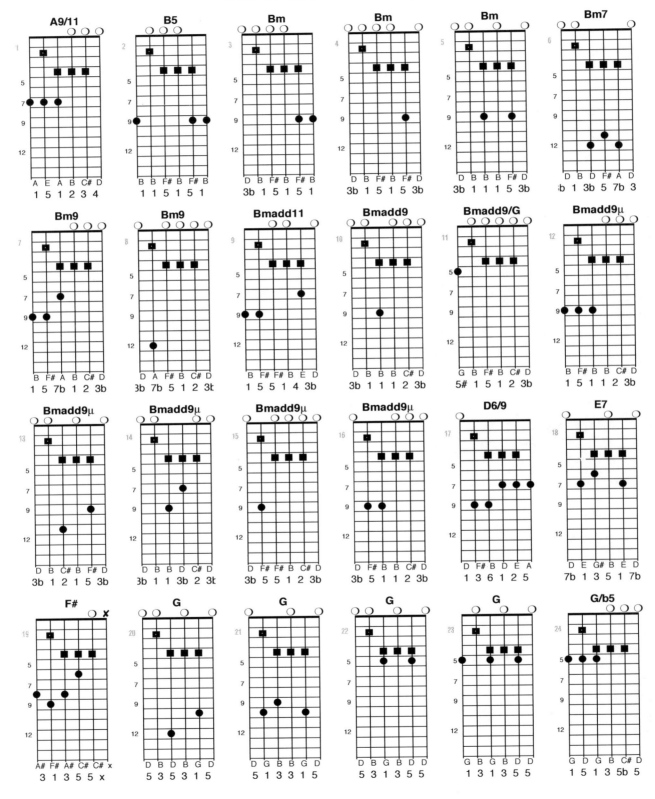

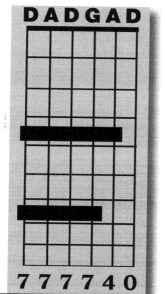

 # 21- 777740

This one is a variation of an earlier (#18) single-capo configuration. It offers some wonderful new sounds on the treble end. Just like the 777700 situation, this does a number of things for you: 1) It puts you in the key of A, 2) it changes the timbre of the guitar from the low sound of the DADGAD tuning to an airier, brighter one 3) it gives you a new library of harp-like open-string scale options on the treble strings; and 4) it also offers a fresh batch of the overlapping, close-voiced "*mu*" chords (p. 14) where you have the 2 and 3, 3 and 4 or 5 and 6 of the scales sounding simultaneously on adjacent strings in the same octave. In fact, the top 3 strings sound the 4-3-4 notes of the scale which means the open chord is an A chord with an added 4th (also called an 11th), more like the familiar *sus4* sound of the DADGAD tuning itself than the previous configuration.

Again, because DADGAD has a "spelling" of 1-5-1 on the bottom three strings, you can play 2 and 2m chords (in this case, B and Bm family) and have a nice low end for the chords. As in the previous situation, 2 chords are not often readily available in the world of partial capoing, and it's nice to be able to use them. The Bm gets an added 9th with the "*mu*" effect, which when arpeggiated is really a striking sound.

You might be able to do this on most guitars by just offsetting two straight capos, since fingerboards tend to get wider as you go up the neck. You could probably do the upper capo with a *Shubb c8b, G7 Newport* or *Kyser Drop D* capo that is designed for 5 strings.

The best way to do it is with a pair of *Planet Waves Trios*, or just the *Trio* for the upper capo and an offset standard capo below. You can of course use a universal capo, but there are some nice chords that use some notes that are under and behind the capos.

A *Planet Waves Trio* capo at the 7th fret and an offset *Planet Waves NS* full capo at the 2nd fret making the 777740 configuration.

777740

Some Chords in the DADGAD 7 7 7 7 4 0 Configuration p.1
TUNING: DADGAD

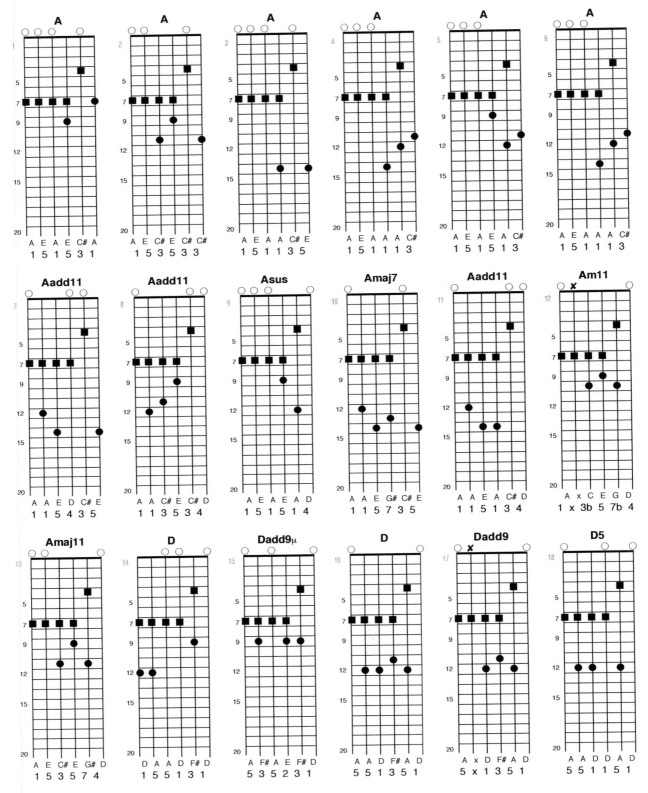

Some Chords in the DADGAD 7 7 7 7 4 0 Configuration p.2
TUNING: DADGAD

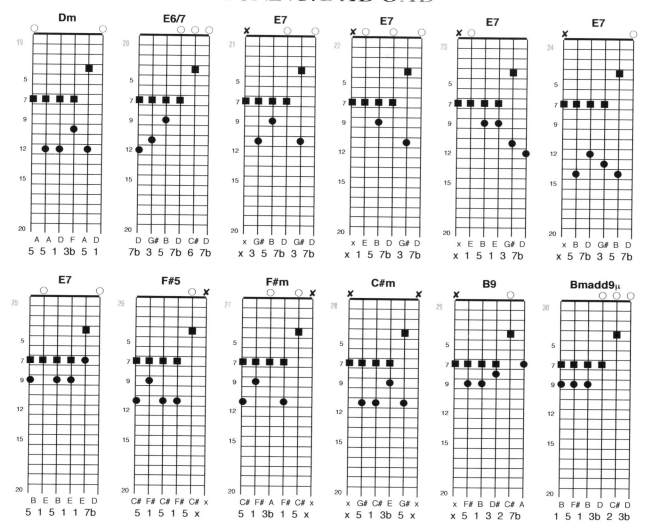

SUSPENDED AND 11TH CHORDS

The *suspended* chord (which is sometimes called *suspended 4th*, and written *sus* or *sus4*) is an important chord in guitar, and it is especially relevant to the partial capo because so many of the widely-used capo configurations involve suspended chords. It usually resolves back to the 1, but it can be a bridge to the 4 chord also. "Officially" a "suspended 4" chord has a 4 but not a 3, and if they are both present in the same octave it is often called an "*add11*" chord, which better describes the chord structure. The 4th and an 11th are the same note name. "Officially" an 11th chord also has a 7th and a 9th, but since there are 6 notes in a full 11th chord, there are few of them on guitar that aren't missing some of the 6 notes. It is not clear always when to call it *11* or *add11*.

Even this gets fuzzy when there may be a 4 in one octave and a 3 and a 4 in another. Is it a suspended 4 with an added 11? You decide, because I can't. There are some chords I have labeled *sus* that you might want to call *add11* and vice versa. Don't sweat it, or call the "chord police."

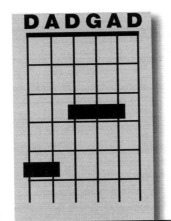

22- 553330

This is a variation of configuration #16 (p. 49,) and it offers some new opportunities, and is well worth exploring. You will need a second partial capo to do it, and many types of common partial capos can do the lower of the 2 capos. You could use a 3-string *Esus* capo attached from the treble side, though it would block access to the high E string below the capo, or if you had a *Kyser K-Lever "Open G"* (white) capo it would work great, since those attach from the bass side and clamp strings 2-3-4. A five string shortened capo attached from the bass side, or just an offset full capo generally can also do the job, as shown in the photo.

The bottom two strings capoed to fret 5 work like configuration #21, and they also move your best key center from D to G. The addition of the second capo opens up a nice set of possibilities, especially because it offers flowing harp-like scales and close-voiced chords well suited to fingerpicking. The top 3 open strings now are just a whole step apart, and because the 3rd string is now sounding a B♭, it makes this configuration particularly suited to playing in Gm or modal tonalities with a flatted 3rd scale note.

You'll notice there are a lot of Gm chords in the chart, and the open C and D notes on the top add a useful 1 on your 2nd string and a 2 note (same as the 9th) on the high string to the C family of chords.

The chord charts here don't show the scale possibilities, and if you have some skills in DADGAD tuning, you'll have a good time here exploring ways to weave flowing scale passages in and among the new landscape of open strings.

A *Woodie's G-Band Model 2* and an offset *Planet Waves NS* full capo making a 553330 configuration in DADGAD tuning.

The upper capo has to be a *Woodie's G-Band Model 2*, but the lower one can be any number of common partial capos or even a standard capo offset as shown. If you use a *Kyser K-Lever* WHITE or a *Liberty "Flip"* you'll be able to access the high E string at the 2nd fret if you need to.

553330

Some Chords in the DADGAD 553330 Configuration p.1
TUNING: DADGAD

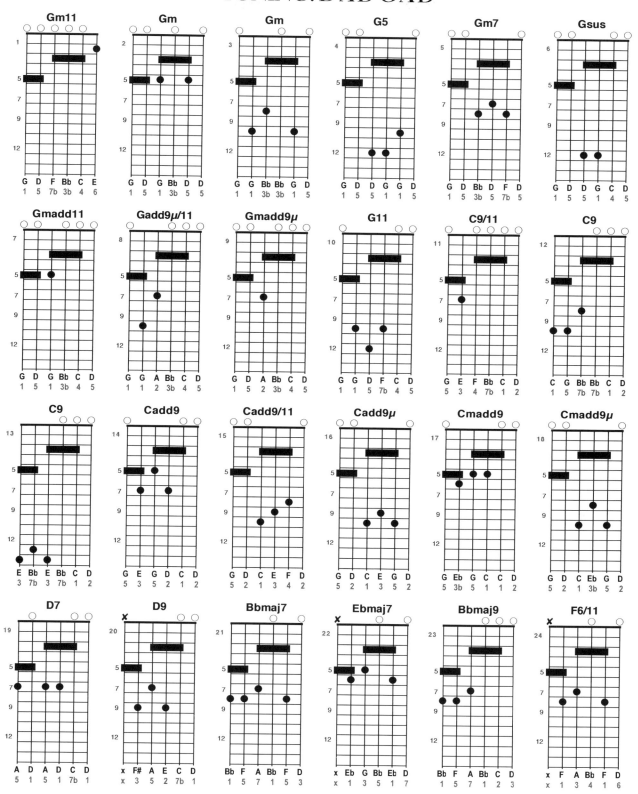

23 - 550030

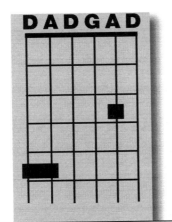

An "exotic" variation on the previous DADGAD capo configuration (and on #15,) this one has some charms of its own, particularly for fingerpicking or arpeggiated chording. You'll need a Model 2 *G-Band* to capo the bass end, and a modified Model 2 (notched out to clamp only the B string) on the treble side. You could of course try it first with universal capos and get a sense of how good it sounds before cutting up capos.

The idea here is that your key center is G, and you have a 1-5-5-1 on the low end, which is bass support for playing in all forms of the G scales. The second capo adds a number of advantages.

Not having the B^b open string (like in the previous example) allows you more flexibility, since you could play in G, Gm and modal tonalities based on G. Having a 4th (C note) on the 2nd string means that the open strings sound a Gsus chord, giving some of that suspended tuning/ Esus capo "mojo" that users of DADGAD tuning should already be quite familiar with. In addition, having the C-D notes on adjacent strings on the treble end mean that you can easily find flowing harp-like scales on the top strings, especially when you play on the 3rd string a little higher up the neck.

You'll also find some nice "showy" moves that straddle the single-string capo, since the 2nd fret E of the high string is a useful note, and there are also some nice things you can do between the capos on strings 3 and 4.

The upper capo again has to be a *Woodie's G-Band Model 2*, and the lower one could be a universal, but it still would block a lot of things. You really need to notch out a second *Woodie's Model 2* so that it clamps only the 2nd string.

A *Woodie's G-Band Model 2* and a modified *Woodie's Model 2* making a 550030 configuration in DADGAD tuning

PARTIAL CAPOS IN HISTORY

Capos have existed for centuries, but the partial capo surprisingly has not been a part of guitar playing until the last 30 years or so. I have done some historical research, and have concluded that at least a few people knew about partial capos in parts of Europe in the early 1800's, and produced the only instruments ever made with built-in mechanisms. I have posted an article in the capo history section at *www.partialcapo.com* about this fascinating historical mystery.

If you find the idea of a partial capo confusing, you are in good company. Once you get used to it, it becomes obvious. But something has kept millions of guitarists from using this rather simple and quite useful idea for centuries. That's the biggest mystery, since different tunings have been used all along by everyone.

550030

Some Chords in the DADGAD 550030 Configuration p.1
TUNING: DADGAD

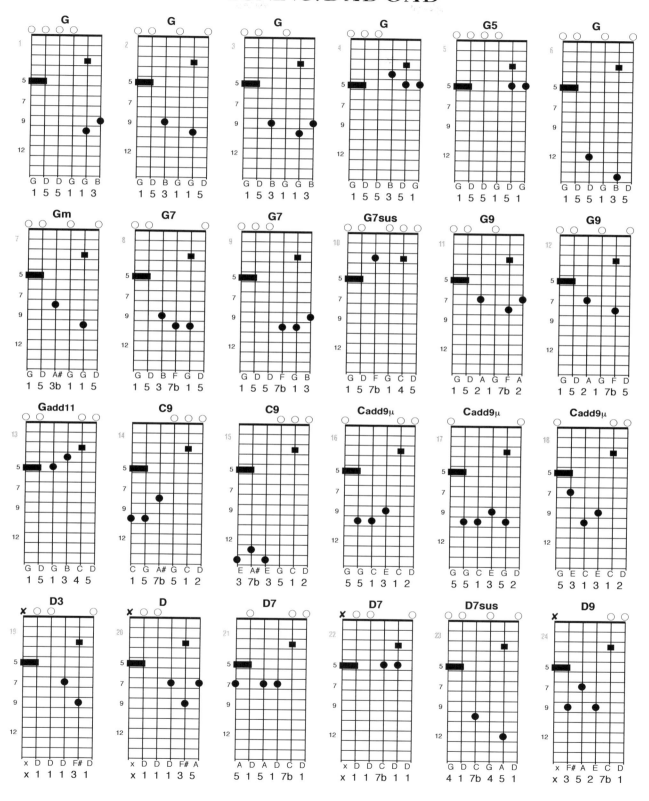

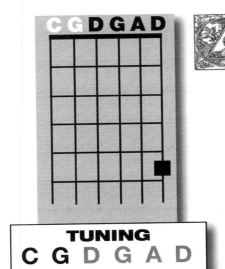

24 ~ High G- Low C [CGDGAD]

Since we have been exploring DADGAD tuning, and we looked at a way to use DADGAD to emulate the lesser-known CGDGAD tuning, we might as well investigate some things we can do in that tuning also. This tuning is a variation on DADGAD, with the bottom 2 strings dropped 2 frets lower. It is gaining steadily in fans, and does not appear to be a fad or something that is going to disappear. It was possibly invented in England in the 1960's by guitarist Dave Evans, and has been popular among American Celtic guitarists, particularly El McMeen, who has played nearly exclusively in this tuning for quite a number of years.

The primary features of the tuning are the low bass and the musical proximity of the open strings on the treble end, in particular, the 2-fret interval between the 2nd and 3rd strings, which is shared by DADGAD tuning. It is particularly useful for playing cascading melodies, where successive notes are on different strings, which give a harp-like sound.

It is not what I think of as an "intuitive" tuning, though it does offer the ability to play in more than one key, which sets it apart from a number of common tunings. The fact that the top 4 strings are the same as DADGAD tuning means that players used to that tuning can at least play on the top 4 strings the same way they are used to doing.

*A **Woodie's G-Band Model 1** making a High G-Low C configuration.*

Tune 6th string down 2 more frets to C

Tune 5th string down 2 more frets to G

Adding partial capos to this tuning allows another new set of possibilities, and illustrates again why even people who use different tunings a lot should also explore the use of the partial capo.

This one adds a high G drone, which is welcome, given the low overall pitch of this tuning. The same kinds of things that make a banjo's 5th string appealing work here. Since a lot of the melodic work in this tuning takes place on the middle strings, it does not interfere with the tuning by tying up the 1st string with the capo the way it would in DADGAD tuning.

The only practical way to do this is with a Woodie's G-Band Model 1, since all other partial capos will block too much of the fingerboard.

0 0 0 0 0 5

Some Chords in the High G - "Low C" Tuning p.1
TUNING: ("Low C") C G D G A D

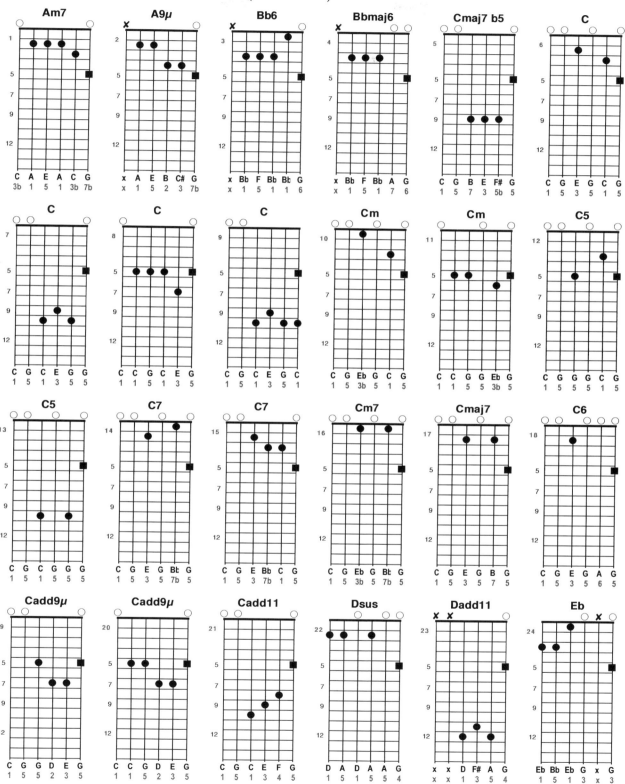

Some Chords in the High G - "Low C" Tuning p.2
TUNING: ("Low C") C G D G A D

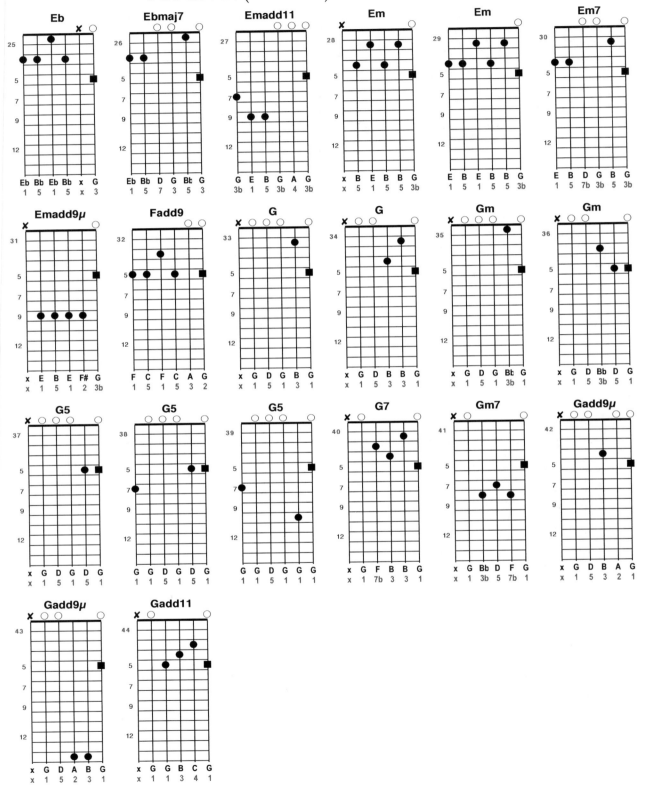

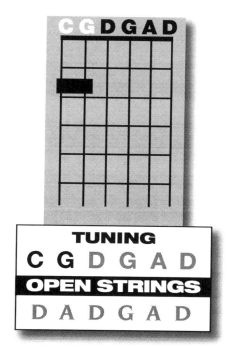

25- "Add-Gad" 220000 [CGDGAD]

In this configuration we use the partial capo to "return" the CGDGAD tuning to DADGAD tuning by bringing the bottom strings back up 2 frets. (Notice that the open strings now sound an open DADGAD chord.) The *Woodie's G-Band Model 2* does the job much better than a universal capo, and allows access to critical areas of the fingerboard that would be blocked by a universal capo. You may have trouble with anything thicker than light gauge strings, since the capo tends to slip out of position, and you may not be able to count on it for a concert performance depending on how the *Woodie's Model 2* fits your fingerboard.

If you are already going to be in this tuning, you might as well work up a few songs this way if you can, since it allows playing in D rather than C and G, and helps avoid some of the inevitable monotony of any tuning.

There are enough similarities to the familiar territory of both DADGAD and the CGDGAD tunings to make it both inviting and confusing, and the same kinds of harp-like voicings and arpeggiated chords that both tunings allow are still available, and in this case only the bass notes are changed.

You still have a nice bass sound, and the plaintive suspended 4th sound that DADGAD tuning and the *Esus* capo both give you is more apparent here.

The only practical way to do this is with a *Woodie's G-Band Model 2*, since all other partial capos will block too much of the fingerboard. You may have trouble getting the *G-Band* to clamp properly, which is too bad, since this is a useful configuration.

A *Woodie's G-Band Model 2* making the Low C "Add-Gad" configuration.

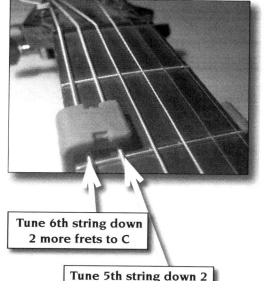

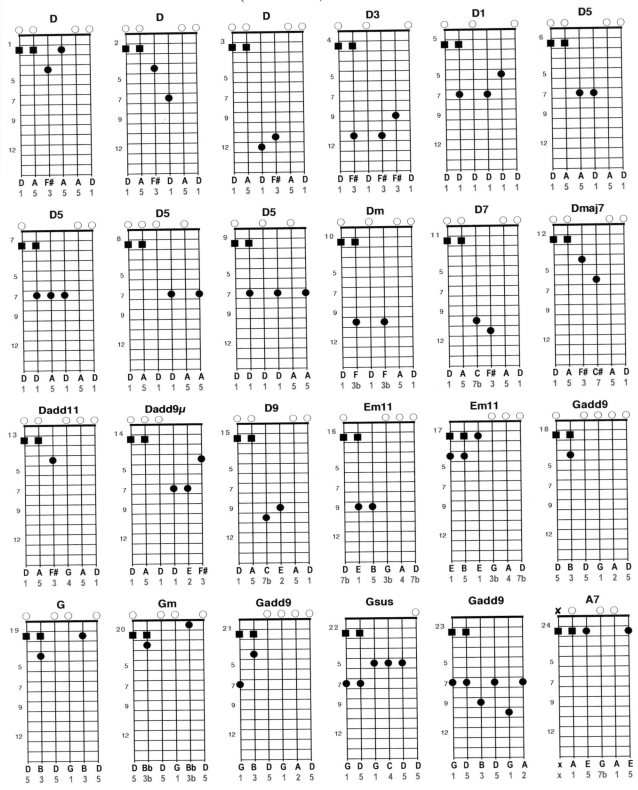

Some Chords in the "ADD-GAD" 220000 Configuration p.2
TUNING: ("Low C") C G D G A D

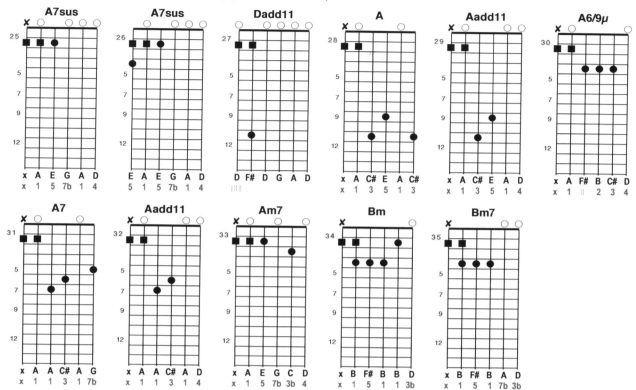

ABOUT PARTIAL CAPO MECHANISMS

People have been trying for years to make a better and a truly universal partial capo. Existing capos are still a bit clumsy and obtrusive. The single-purpose partial capos are less visible and not as much in the way, but they are not perfect designs either. The *Shubb c7b* and the *Kyser Short-Cut* "Esus" capos, that clamp 3 inner strings, are too big for narrow necks like *Fender* electrics, and too small for classical necks or 12-strings. Ideally, there should be three models of the *Esus* capo to accommodate all the widths of fingerboards. Since it only clamps 3 strings, the *Esus* capo does not need to compensate for fingerboard radius, which can be a problem with longer capos.

Making a perfect partial capo is a harder problem than it seems at a glance. There is a huge range of string gauges, action, neck widths, thicknesses and shapes among the guitars of the world. String height at the 12th fret can be high, so capos end up being bulky in order to have clearance for all scenarios. Building a mechanism into the guitar seems to make sense, but there are not many players yet who are willing to drill holes and modify their guitars when they can accomplish the same thing with capos that can easily be moved to other frets or to other instruments.

The *Third Hand* rotating cam mechanism has been around since 1976, and in 2008 when Peter Einhorn made the new design called the *SpiderCapo*, it still had the same basic drawbacks as the *Third Hand*: it blocks access to the fingerboard, and is very visible. Both capos adjust for string spacing, though the *SpiderCapo* doesn't accommodate 12-strings or very curved fingerboards, and needs a special model for classical width necks.

26~ 055555 [CGDGAD]

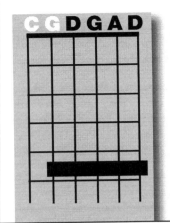

This capo configuration does a couple useful things: It retains the deep C-G bass of this tuning, while raising the pitch and brightening the timbre of the guitar. As is the case with a lot of tunings, there is always a danger of monotony, and a quick way like this to change the sound without changing the tuning should be welcome. If you sing in this tuning, it is extra useful.

The double-octave C in the bass is a striking feature of this configuration, and it makes it hard to play in keys other than C or F. The next configuration is only slightly different, and each of them has strengths and weaknesses built around what happens on the 5th string.

You can easily do this with the *Planet Waves Trio* or the *Planet Waves Dual-Action*, or with a *Shubb c8b* , *G7 Newport* or *Kyser Drop D* capo that is designed for 5 strings. You could also use a universal capo, since there are no chords shown here that use notes beside or behind the capo. You can almost certainly do this also by just offsetting a full capo.

A ***Planet Waves Dual-Action*** *capo at the 5th fret leaving the bass string unclamped.*

Tune 6th string down 2 more frets to C

Tune 5th string down 2 more frets to G

0 5 5 5 5 5

Some Chords in the CGDGAD 055555 Configuration p.1
TUNING: C G D G B E

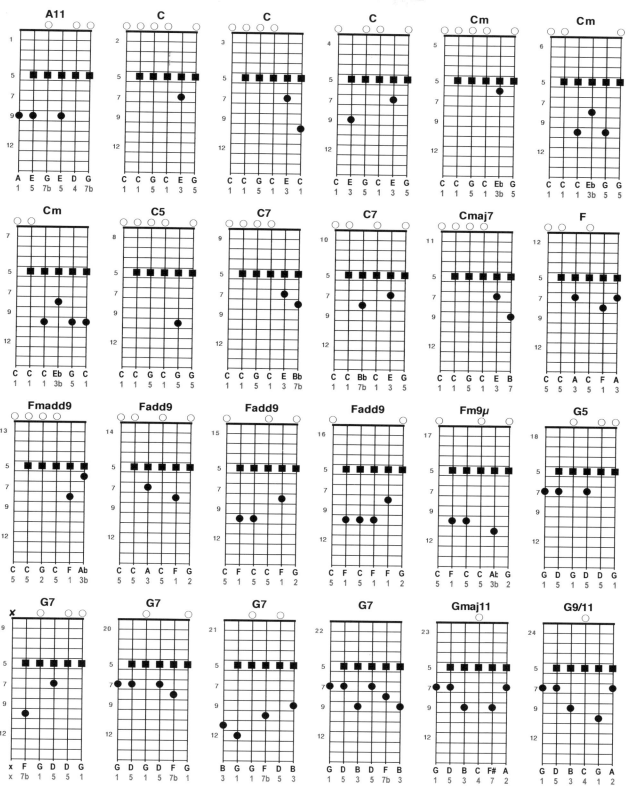

27 - 005555 [CGDGAD]

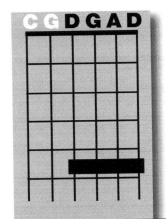

Tune 6th string down 4 frets to C, 5th string down 2 to G

While we are looking at ways to use a shortened capo in CGDGAD tuning, we might as well look at a final one, which is just a little different than the previous one because the 5th string is now open to the nut. The open strings form a *Cadd9µ* chord, which is a nice starting point. The top 4 strings are tuned just like DADGAD, so capo 5 just moves things up to a Gsus open chord. Though it is harder to get used to than the previous 055555 configuration, it is probably more musically useful overall, and there are some great new possibilities here.

Here we have the ability to play in G, unlike the previous situation with the double-C bass, but we still retain the very low bass sound that is a hallmark of this tuning. Adding the capo brightens the treble end considerably, and the combination of low bass and high treble, as we saw in some previous examples, is always appealing and makes a very full sound.

The best way to do it is with the *Planet Waves Trio* or the *Planet Waves Dual-Action*. You could also use a universal capo, since there are no chords shown here that use notes under or behind the capo. You might be able to do this by just offsetting a straight capo, since fingerboards tend to get wider as you go up the neck. You can probably do it with a *Shubb c8b*, *G7 Newport*, *Liberty "Flip"* or *Kyser Drop D* capo that is designed for 5 strings.

A ***Planet Waves Trio*** *capo at the 5th fret leaving 2 bass strings unclamped.*

0 0 **5 5 5 5**

Some Chords in the CGDGAD 005555 Configuration p.1
TUNING: C G D G B E

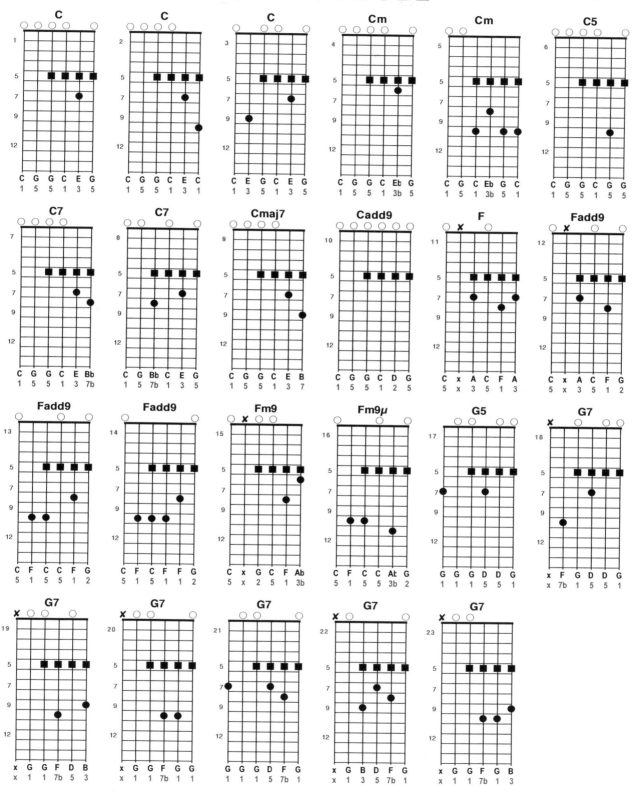

Appendix: DADGAD Tuning & the Esus Partial Capo

How the "simulated DADGAD" capo configuration compares to DADGAD tuning

E-Suspended (Esus)

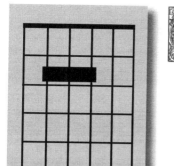

TUNING
E A D G B E
OPEN STRINGS
E B E A B E

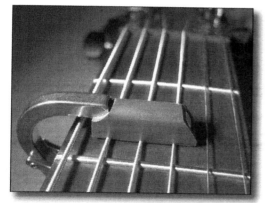

A Shubb c7b capo forming the Esus configuration in standard tuning.

Esus (usually pronounced "E-suss") is short for *"E-Suspended,"* the chord formed by the partial capo. I first did this in about 1980, and it has become the most common standard tuning partial capo configuration. It generates an "open-tuned" sound that is often confused with DADGAD tuning. (Eric Schoenberg whimsically called it *"Faux-Gad"* tuning.) I have included this section in the book, in case you are a DADGAD player who has never tried the *Esus* capo in standard tuning. Hopefully this will clarify some of the confusion about the similarities and differences of the two "tunings," and entice some players who have not tried *Esus* to give it a try. They are not at all the same, and both have equal but different value.

There is a lot of confusion among players of all levels about the differences and similarities between DADGAD tuning and an *Esus* capo. Two of the makers of *Esus* capos even call it a "DADGAD capo" which is quite misleading. In DADGAD, strings 1, 2 and 6 are lowered 2 frets from standard tuning. With an *Esus* capo, the other 3 strings are raised by 2 frets. The kinds of sounds that are available are similar, and each approach gives a similar set of new drone strings, but new chord fingerings and voicings above the capo.

Partial capos are used for the same reasons as new tunings: to change the landscape of possibilities on the fingerboard. It is vital to realize that a tuning is quite different from a partial capo, and the specifics of what scales, notes, chords you can play are completely different, since the guitar is not tuned the same in both situations, and only seems to be. Only things you play on only strings 1-2-6 will finger the same.

The *Esus* environment lets you combine standard tuning chord and scale patterns with your new set of open strings, and you always retain the option of playing closed-position scales or barre chords above the capo. You also can choose to sound like an open tuning, or to sound like standard tuning, and in the same song you can go in an out of an open-tuning sound. **It is not really an option in DADGAD tuning to sound like standard tuning.**

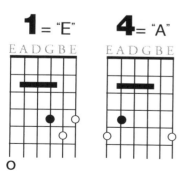

- These fingerings allow you to make 1, 4 & 5 chords in the key of E with only one finger. The white dots show optional fingerings (that just form regular D, G and A chords.)
- Only one string is muted in all three chords. (The bass E string is muted on the 5 chord)
- The chord names are shown in quotes because they are actually E^5, A^{add9} and B^{7sus} chords, which function like E, A and B7 chords in most songs. The extra notes in them actually sound better than "normal" chords in a lot of songs, though in other songs they may not suit your tastes.

0 2 2 2 0 0

Comparison of Esus chords to DADGAD Tuning p. 1

Esus chords with partial capo are shown on a standard-guitar tuned down 2 frets to D-G-C-F-A-D

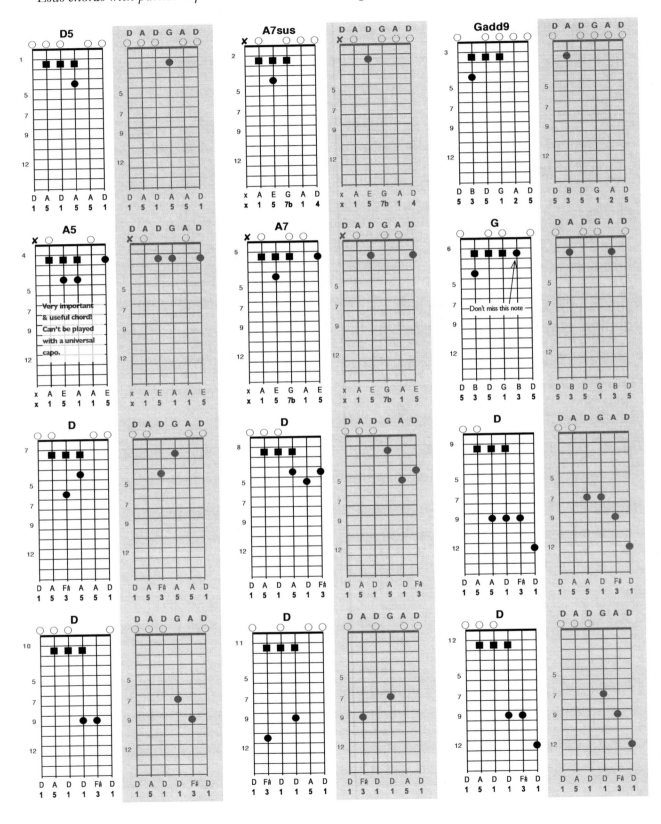

Comparison of Esus chords to DADGAD Tuning p. 2

Esus chords with partial capo are shown on a standard-guitar tuned down 2 frets to D-G-C-F-A-D

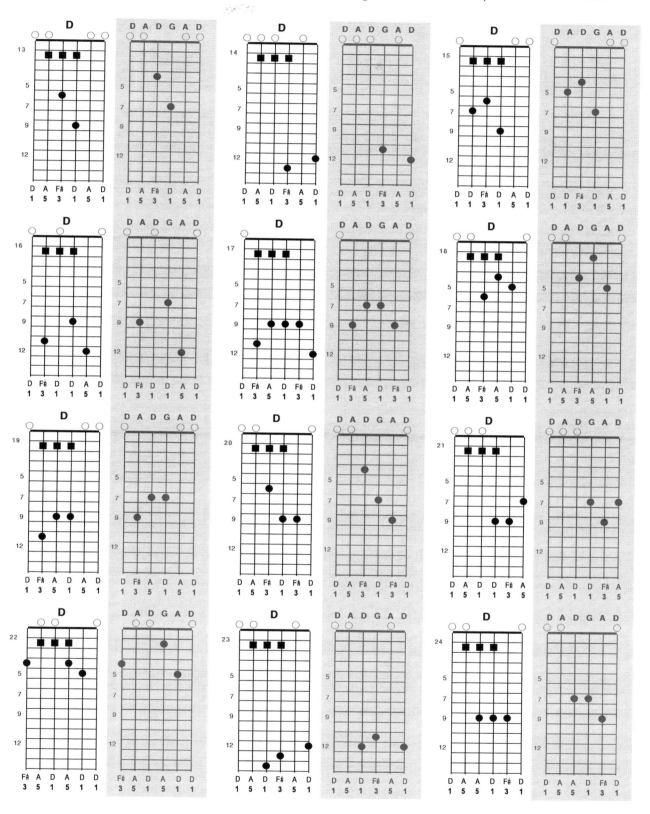

Comparison of Esus chords to DADGAD Tuning p. 3

Esus chords with partial capo are shown on a standard-guitar tuned down 2 frets to D-G-C-F-A-D

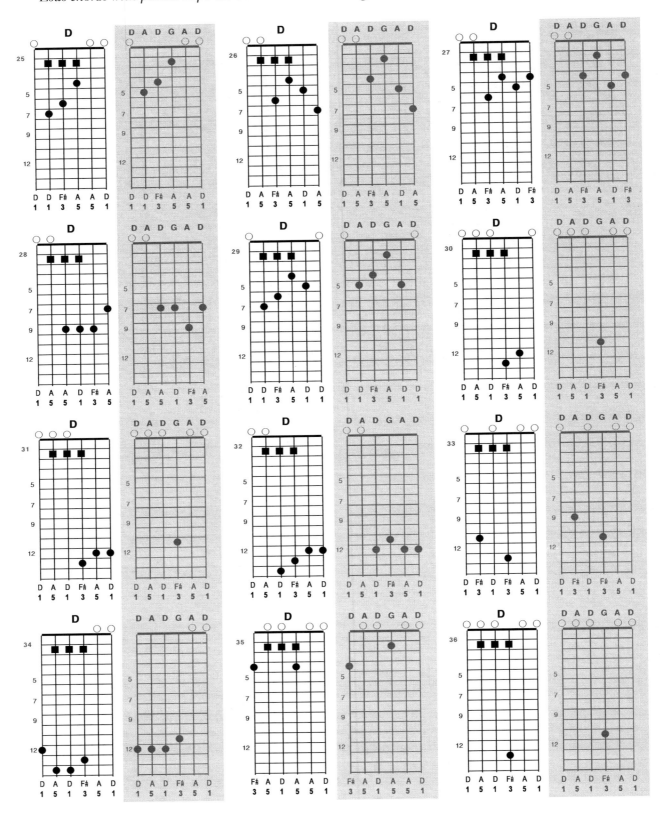

Comparison of Esus chords to DADGAD Tuning p. 4

Esus chords with partial capo are shown on a standard-guitar tuned down 2 frets to D-G-C-F-A-D

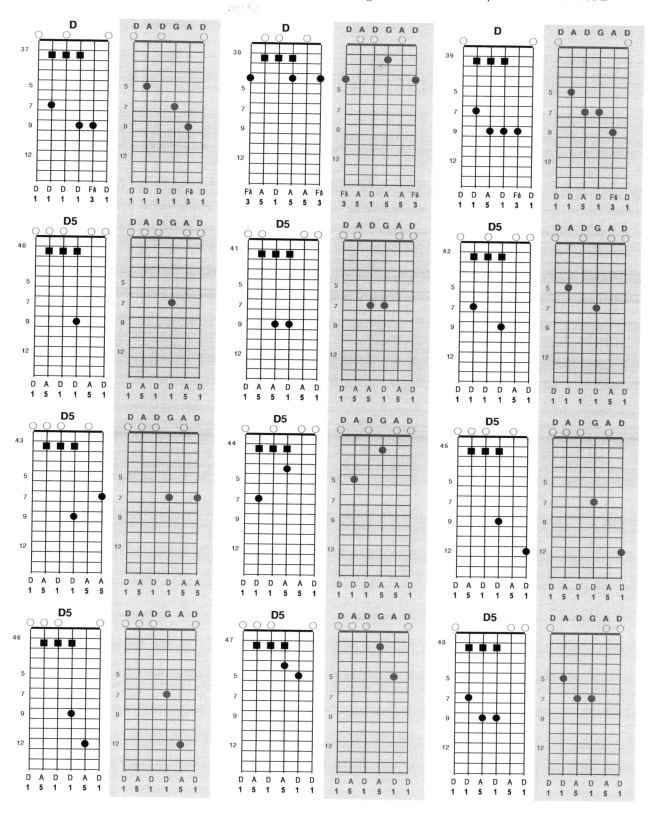

Comparison of Esus chords to DADGAD Tuning p. 5

Esus chords with partial capo are shown on a standard guitar tuned down 2 frets to D-G-C-F-A-D

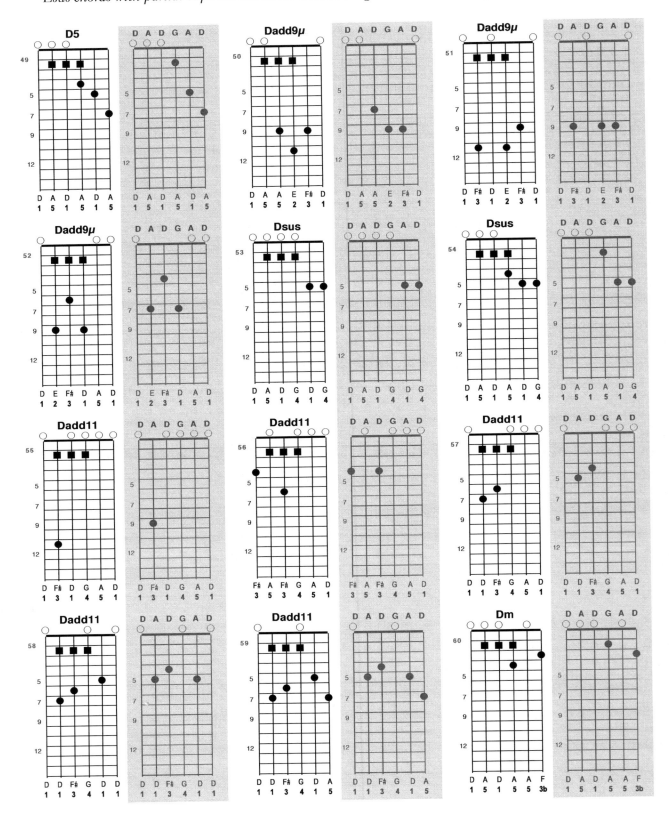

Comparison of Esus chords to DADGAD Tuning p. 6

Esus chords with partial capo are shown on a standard-guitar tuned down 2 frets to D-G-C-F-A-D

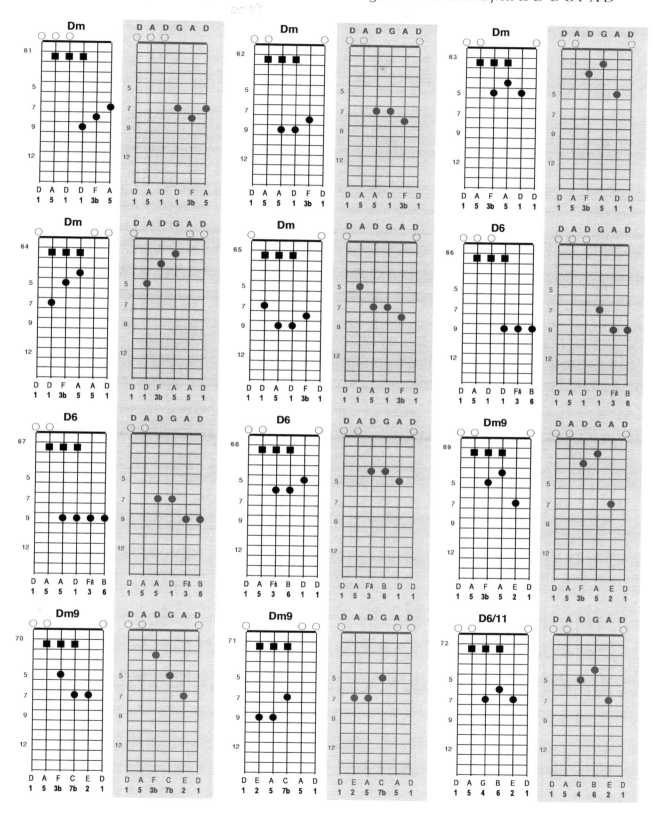

Comparison of Esus chords to DADGAD Tuning p. 7

Esus chords with partial capo are shown on a standard-guitar tuned down 2 frets to D-G-C-F-A-D

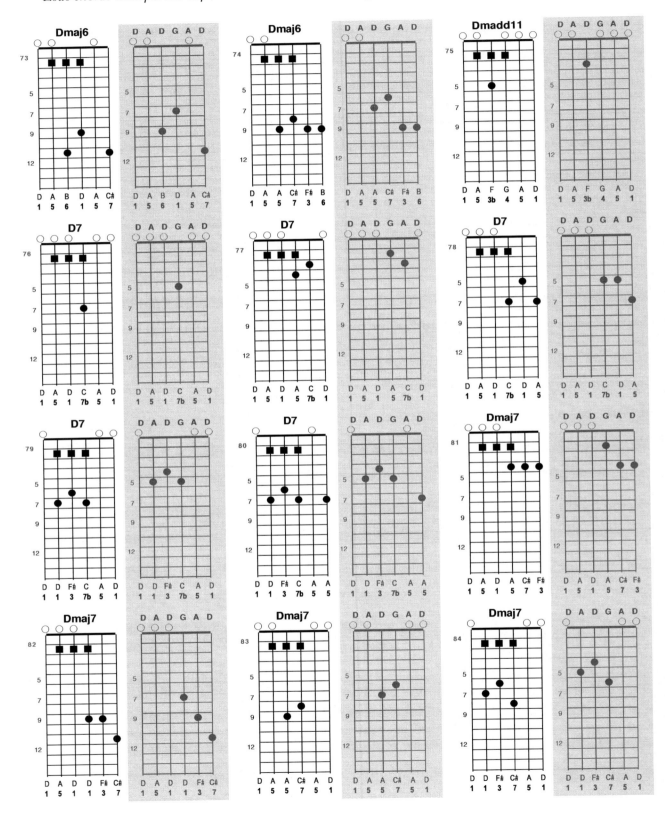

Comparison of Esus chords to DADGAD Tuning p. 8

Esus chords with partial capo are shown on a standard-guitar tuned down 2 frets to D-G-C-F-A-D

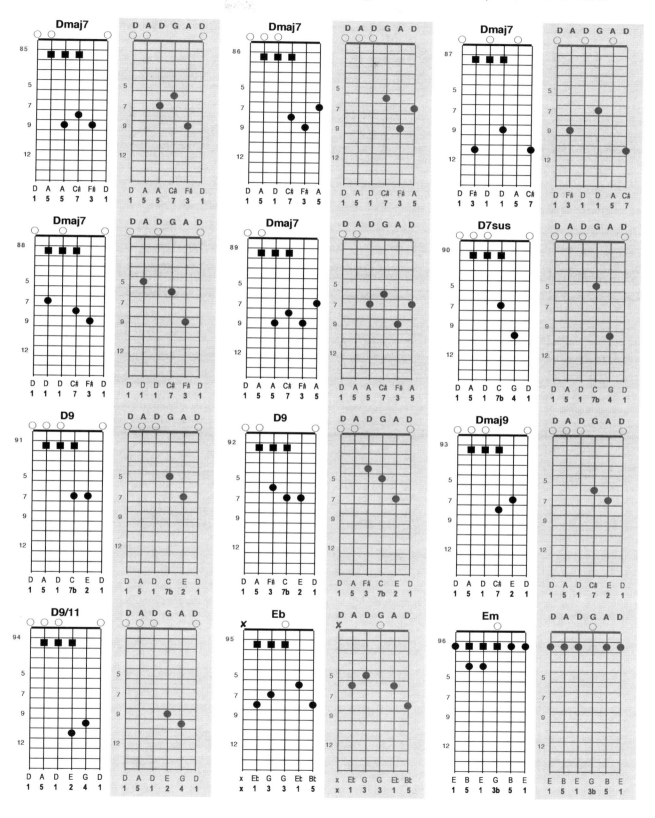

Comparison of Esus chords to DADGAD Tuning p. 9

Esus chords with partial capo are shown on a standard-guitar tuned down 2 frets to D-G-C-F-A-D

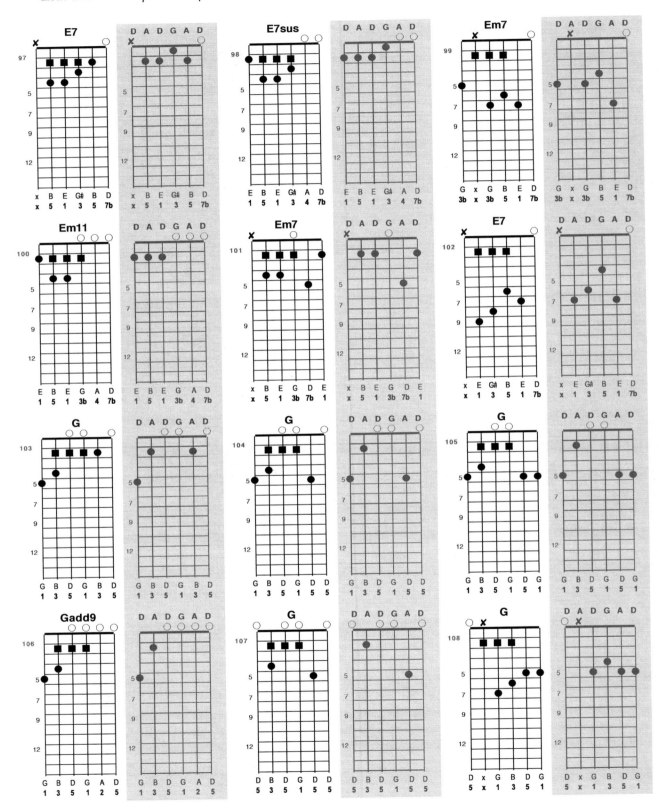

Comparison of Esus chords to DADGAD Tuning p.10

Esus chords with partial capo are shown on a standard-guitar tuned down 2 frets to D-G-C-F-A-D

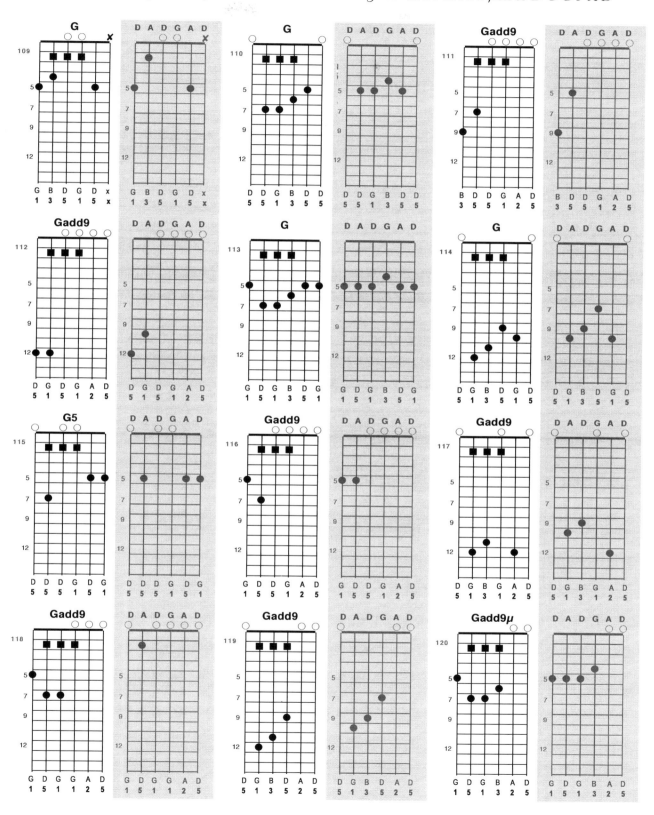

Comparison of Esus chords to DADGAD Tuning p.11

Esus chords with partial capo are shown on a standard-guitar tuned down 2 frets to D-G-C-F-A-D

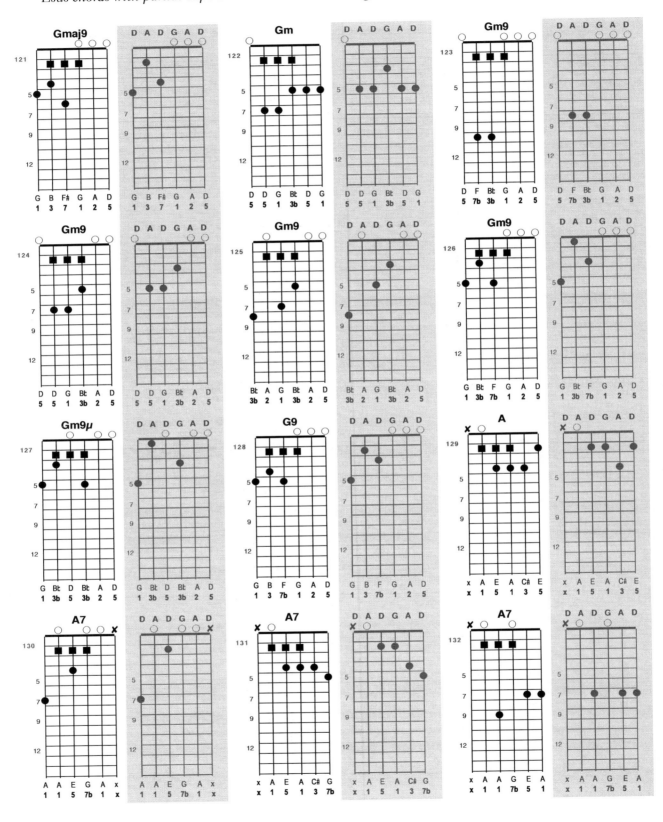

Comparison of Esus chords to DADGAD Tuning p.12

Esus chords with partial capo are shown on a standard-guitar tuned down 2 frets to D-G-C-F-A-D

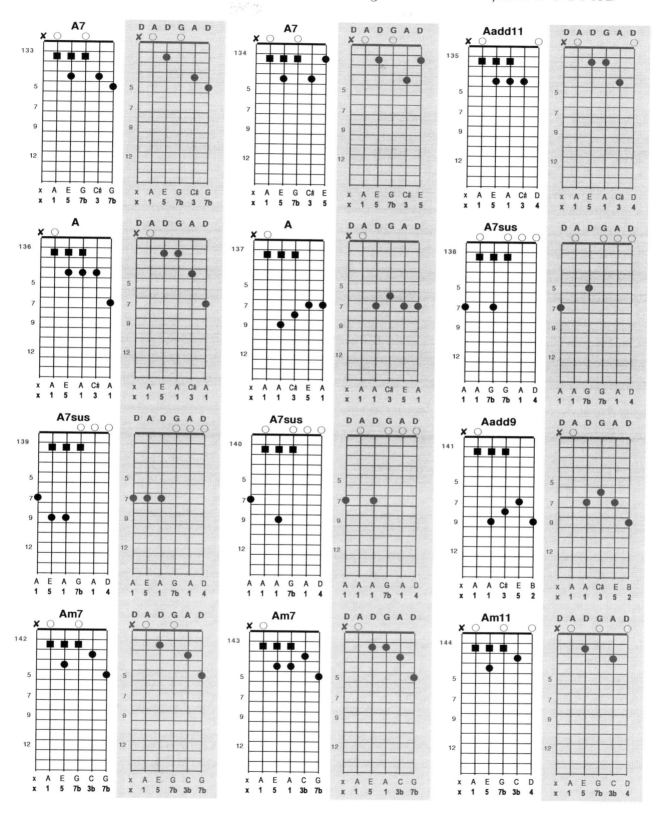

Comparison of Esus chords to DADGAD Tuning p.13

Esus chords with partial capo are shown on a standard-guitar tuned down 2 frets to D-G-C-F-A-D

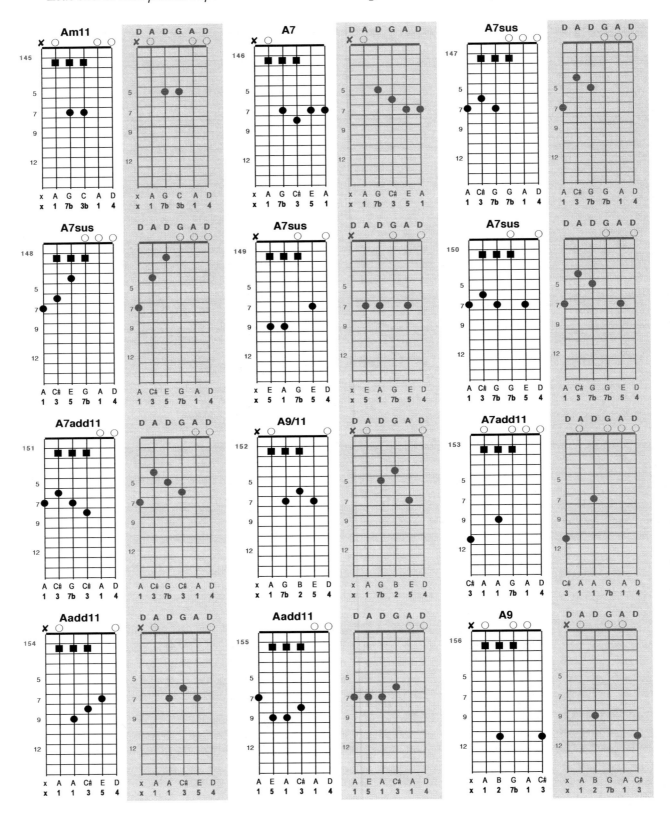

Comparison of Esus chords to DADGAD Tuning p.14

Esus chords with partial capo are shown on a standard-guitar tuned down 2 frets to D-G-C-F-A-D

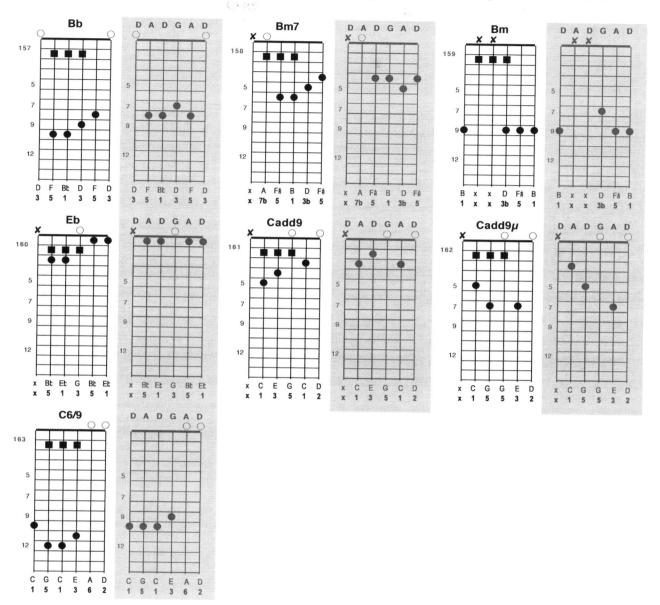

ESUS CAPO VS. DADGAD TUNING

Esus has one distinct disadvantage, which is that very little traditional music is played in the key of E. D is a very crucial key for both guitarists and singers, especially those who play along with fiddles, mandolins, dulcimers and other traditional instruments. If the key of D is essential for you, try using heavier-gauge (such as medium) string and tune the whole guitar down 2 frets, which will also give you the slack-string tone that is such a part of the DADGAD sound. Your other option is to get a baritone guitar, many of which have scale lengths that are exactly 2 frets longer than a regular guitar. You could then capo 2 and be at standard pitch, and when you play *Esus* capo music you will be pitched the same as DADGAD tuning.

More Musical Resources By Harvey Reid

THE SONG TRAIN (2007) is a landmark resource for beginning guitarists by Harvey Reid & Joyce Andersen. 4-CD boxed set with 80-page color hardback book, contains 56 one & two chord songs. Half the songs are copyrighted, by the likes of Bob Dylan, Hank Williams, Chuck Berry etc, so it offers beginners easy but great songs they can play. Folk, blues, gospel, rock, celtic, country and gospel songs, and an amazing cross-section of American music. **www.songtrain.net**

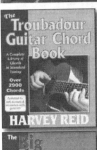

THE TROUBADOUR GUITAR CHORD BOOK (2013) The best, most complete and readable standard-tuning chord encyclopedia, and an essential new reference tool. A monumental and important new work that may never go back on your shelf. Unlike other large chord books that are tailored for jazz guitarists, the *Troubadour Guitar Chord Book* features over 2900 open and closed-string voicings, optimized and selected for solo acoustic and troubadour-style guitarists.

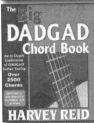

THE BIG DADGAD CHORD BOOK (2014) The best, most complete and readable chord encyclopedia in DADGAD tuning, with 2500 chords mapped out. Another indispensable reference book for anyone who plays in this popular tuning. Also features full-fingerboard diagrams, with every note and scale degree shown for every chord.

THE BIG BOOK OF BANJO CHORDS (2015) The most complete, detailed and versatile book of chords for standard banjo G tuning. The fingerboard shown like never before, with 5th string notes shown.

THE BIG BOOK OF MANDOCELLO CHORDS (2015) The most complete, detailed & versatile book (over 2000 chords) for standard C-G-A-D tuning. Includes the first ideas ever published for partial capos on mandocello.

THE BIG BOOK OF BARITONE UKULELE CHORDS (2015) The most complete, detailed and versatile book of chords for standard D-G-B-E tuning. Over 2100 chords, including some new partial capo ideas.

BARITONE UKULELE SIMPLIFIED (2015) Explores 9 different new tunings and partial capo ideas that reveal for the first time how to play instant music with great-sounding but simpler chord shapes.

SLEIGHT OF HAND (1983) The first book of partial capo guitar arrangements, still in print. 16 solo guitar arrangements using a universal partial capo. Intermediate to advanced level, mostly for fingerstyle guitar, but has 2 flatpicked fiddle tune arrangements (*Sally Goodin'* and *Devil's Dream*) In TAB and standard notation. *Suite: For the Duchess, Für Elise, Scarborough Fair, Minuet in Dm, Flowers of Edinburgh, Simple Gifts, Sally Goodin', Irish Washerwoman, Pavanne, Minuet in Dm, Red-Haired Boy, June Apple, Jesu Joy of Man's Desiring, Devil's Dream, Sally Goodin', Scherzo, Shenandoah, Greensleeves, Sailor's Hornpipe, Fisher's Hornpipe*

CAPO INVENTIONS (2006) 14 intermediate to advanced arrangements from Reid's catalog of guitar recordings. Precisely transcribed for solo guitar, these pieces all use a 3-string *Esus* type partial capo. In TAB and standard notation. *Skye Boat Song, Highwire Hornpipe, Windy Grave, Hard Times, The Unknown Soldier, Suite: For the Duchess, The Arkansas Traveler, The Minstrel Boy, Red in the Sky, Prelude to the Minstrel's Dream, Norway Suite: Parts 1 &2, Star Island Jig, Macallan's Jig.*

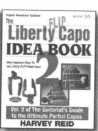

THE LIBERTY "FLIP" CAPO IDEA BOOKS (2014-15) Two volumes, totaling almost 400 pages, with over 113 ideas of partial capo configurations that can be done with a pair of *Model 43* and *Model 65 Liberty* partial capos. These were developed by Harvey Reid, and are the new generation of sleek and versatile partial capos that clamp 6, 5, 4 or 3 strings on most guitars, banjos, ukes and mandolins. Volume I shows 72 ideas, mostly in standard tuning, and with a taste of combining capos with altered tunings. Volume 2 combines capos with altered tunings.

SECRETS OF THE 3-STRING PARTIAL CAPO (2010) 24 mind-bending ways to use the popular 3-string *Esus* (*E-suspended*) type partial capo. *This book may no longer be available after the arrival of the Liberty Capos.* **18 of these ideas are now in the *Liberty Capo IDEA BOOK*, and the other 6 appear in the *Liberty "FLIP" Capo IDEA BOOK Vol.2.***

MORE SECRETS OF THE 3-STRING PARTIAL CAPO (2013) 27 more ways to use 3-string *Esus* (*E-suspended*) type partial capos. **12 of these ideas are now in the *Liberty Capo IDEA BOOK*, and the others are in the *Liberty Capo IDEA BOOK Vol.2.***

SECRETS OF THE 4 & 5-STRING PARTIAL CAPOS (2011) Another treasure trove of ideas, for the *Planet Waves*, *Shubb*, or *Kyser* shortened 4 or 5-string capos. (Also valuable for *Third Hand*, *Liberty "Flip"* or *Spider* universal capos.) Most people who have one of these capos know a few ways to use them. Here are an amazing 47 ideas that use a 4 or 5-string capo to generate new music. Over 1600 chords. *This book may no longer be available after the arrival of the Liberty Capos.* **30 of these 47 ideas are now in the *Liberty Capo IDEA BOOK*, and the other 17 appear in the *Liberty Capo IDEA BOOK Vol.2.***

SECRETS OF THE 1 & 2-STRING PARTIAL CAPOS (2012) How to use the unique *Woodie's G-Band* 1 and 2-string partial capos. 33 clever ways to use these capos in a number of tunings and in combination with other partial capos, with over 1100 chords. 98 pages are packed with photos, ideas and capo knowledge that is only available here. Even the makers of the capos don't know about these ideas.

SECRETS OF PARTIAL CAPOS IN DADGAD TUNING (2012) Most people think of partial capos as a substitute for open tunings, and don't realize that they can be combined. Harvey Reid shows you over 25 ingenious ways to use partial capos to expand the musical possibilities of DADGAD tuning (4 of them use the similar CGDGAD tuning.) Get new chords, fingerings, voicings, resonances and unlock a new, mysterious world of new music hiding in your fingerboard. **17 of these ideas are now in the *Liberty Capo IDEA BOOK Vol.2.***

SECRETS OF UNIVERSAL PARTIAL CAPOS (2012) 45 ways to get new music from your guitar that can only be done with universal partial capos. This hidden world of music in your fingerboard includes a number of tunings and combinations with other partial capos. Over 1500 chords. Packed with photos, clear explanations and capo strategy will save you years of searching. **Because the *Model 43 Liberty* capo clamps 4 middle strings, 13 of these ideas are now duplicated in the *Liberty Capo IDEA BOOKS, Vol. 1-2.***

SECRETS OF PARTIAL CAPOS IN DROP D TUNING (2014) The most common tuning is *Drop D*: D A D G B E, and like any tuning, it can be combined with partial capos to add another dimension to the guitar. This book presents 24 ways to use one or more partial capos of all types to generate more new music. **9 of these ideas are now in the *Liberty Capo IDEA BOOK*, and 7 more appear in *Vol.2*.** The others use a universal or *G-Band* capo.

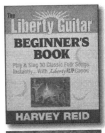

THE LIBERTY GUITAR BEGINNER'S BOOK (2015) Play 30 classic folk songs instantly with super-simple, great-sounding chords. For children or adults, this book carefully explains how to use *Liberty Tuning* to play chords and sing songs in 6 different major and minor keys. You need a guitar, a full capo, and a *Liberty FLIP Model 43* capo.

THE LIBERTY TUNING CHORD BOOK (2013) In his partial capo research, Harvey Reid discovered a simple new guitar tuning that introduces a remarkable geometrical symmetry and simplicity to the guitar fingerboard that no one ever dreamed existed. Here is a thorough examination of what this amazing tuning can do, with over 1200 chords, sorted, mapped out and organized to help you find your way in *Liberty Tuning*. Lots of tips, advice & clear explanations. For guitar teachers, beginners and anyone who already plays guitar and wants to learn about this important discovery.

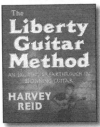

THE LIBERTY GUITAR METHOD (2013) Total beginners can play music like never before. It's easy to do and sounds great. Learn to use *Liberty Tuning* to play great-sounding, simple 2-finger chords to songs by Bob Dylan, Hank Williams, John Prine, Johnny Cash, Chuck Berry, The Beatles, Adele, and more. You won't believe it 'til you try it. *Hush Little Baby, This Land is Your Land, Your Cheating Heart, A Hard Rain's A Gonna Fall, Amazing Grace, The Cuckoo, Folsom Prison Blues, Angel From Montgomery, Maybellene, Let It Be, Imagine, Someone Like You, The Wedding Song, House of the Rising Sun*

THE LIBERTY SONG TRAIN (2013) Learn how to use *Liberty Tuning* to play all 56 two-chord songs in the epic *Song Train* collection with just 2-finger chords, in the same keys as they were done on the *Song Train* recordings. Beginning guitar has never been easier. Careful explanations, with lots of helpful tips, strategy and advice. If you have the *Song Train* 4-CD collection, you need this companion book.

LIBERTY GUITAR FOR KIDS (2013) It's a huge breakthrough in children's guitar. Children as young as 4 can learn to strum simple 2-finger *Liberty Tuning* chords and play guitar like never before. Classic traditional plus modern children's songs arranged in keys young voices can sing in. No need to wait until the children grow bigger or waste your money on crummy small children's guitars. Learn how even small children can instantly start strumming songs on adult guitars. It's really amazing. *London Bridge, Row Row Row Your Boat, Farmer in the Dell, Hush Little Baby, This Land is Your Land, Oh Susannah, Standing in the Need of Prayer, Hey Lolly Lolly, Comin' Round the Mountain* and more.

THE 2-FINGER GUITAR GUIDE (2013) A careful study of simplified guitar chords, this book takes you through each of the common tunings and partial capo configurations that can be used to play simplified guitar chords. Learn the advantages and disadvantages of each of 28 different guitar environments, including the amazing *Liberty Tuning* and related hybrid tunings. If you have a shortage of fingers on the fretting hand, or if you work with hand injuries, special music education or music therapy, this is the definitive guide to showing what can be done musically with just 2 finger chords.

Support Harvey Reid's ground-breaking work in guitar. Buy his books, music, videos, and capos.

www.PartialCapo.com   www.LibertyGuitar.com

Available from Amazon.com and other retail outlets

About the Author

Harvey Reid has been a full-time acoustic guitar player since 1974, and has performed over 6000 concerts throughout the US and in Europe. He won the 1981 *National Fingerpicking Guitar Competition* and the 1982 *International Autoharp* contest, and has released 32 highly-acclaimed recordings of original, traditional and contemporary acoustic music.

He is best known for his solo fingerstyle guitar work, but he is also a solid flatpicker (he won Bill Monroe's *Beanblossom* bluegrass guitar contest in 1976), a versatile singer, lyricist, prolific composer, arranger and songwriter. He also plays mandolin, ukulele, mandocello and bouzouki. Reid recorded the first album ever of 6 & 12-string banjo music, and his CD *Solo Guitar Sketchbook* made GUITAR PLAYER MAGAZINE's Top 20 essential acoustic guitar CD's list. His CD *Steel Drivin' Man* was chosen by ACOUSTIC GUITAR MAGAZINE as one of **Top 10 Folk CD's** of all time, along with Woody Guthrie, Ry Cooder and other hallowed names. His music was included in the blockbuster BBC TV show *A Musical Tour of Scotland*, and Reid was featured in the Rhino Records **Acoustic Music of the 90's** collection, along with a "who's who" line-up of other artists including Richard Thompson, Jerry Garcia & Leo Kottke.

In 1980 Reid published *A New Frontier in Guitar*, the first book about the partial capo, and in 1984 he wrote *Modern Folk Guitar*, the first college textbook for folk guitar. Quite possibly the first modern person to publish and record with the partial capo, he is almost certainly the most prolific arranger and composer of partial capo guitar music, and is responsible for most of what is known about the device. He lives in southern Maine with his family.

Made in the USA
Lexington, KY
28 December 2015